The Wanderer
A Tear and A Smile
Reflections of an Immigrant

RONESA AVEELA

Copyright © 2019 Bendideia Publishing

December 2019

Ebook ISBN: 978-1-949397-97-0
Paperback ISBN: 978-1-949397-89-5
Bulgarian Paperback ISBN: 978-1-949397-96-3

All rights reserved.

All rights reserved. Except for the quotation of short passages for the purposes of criticism and review, no part of this publication may be reproduced, stored in a retrieval system, or transmitted in whole or in part in any form by any electronic, mechanical, or other means, now known or hereafter invented, including xerography, photocopying and recording, without the written permission from the publisher: Bendideia Publishing, www.bendideia.com.

Cover Design by Nelinda, www.nelinda.com.
Illustrations by Nelinda. © Bendideia Publishing.
Editing by Bendideia Publishing.

Contents

Introduction vii
Chapter 1: Faith 1
Chapter 2: Bulgarian Magical Wand 9
Chapter 3: Wine and Love 15
Chapter 4: Martenitsa – a Thread of Hope 23
Chapter 5: Flowers and Love 29
Chapter 6: Proshka – the Art of Forgiveness 35
Chapter 7: Colorful Eggs and Sweet Memories 41
Chapter 8: Name Days – the Season to Cheer 47
Chapter 9: White Roses 53
Chapter 10: Fearless 59
Chapter 11: Horo – the Circle of Love 65
Chapter 12: Samodiva Cheshma – the Magic of Water 71
Chapter 13: Soul of the Bread 77
Chapter 14: Healers of the Soul 85
Chapter 15: Orisia or Choice 91
Chapter 16: Skinny Tulips 99
Chapter 17: The Soul of a Tree 103
Chapter 18: The Gate – Coffee, Cigarettes, and a Drop of Wine 109
Chapter 19: Don't Be Late 115
Author's Note 119
Glossary 123
About the Author 125

All That Is Gold Does Not Glitter

All that is gold does not glitter,
Not all those who wander are lost;
The old that is strong does not wither,
Deep roots are not reached by the frost.

—J. R. R. Tolkien

Introduction

"People have different stars. For those who travel, the stars are the guides. For others, they are only small lights."
—The Little Prince

Throughout history, people have traveled, seeking better conditions. One of the things that distinguishes us from animals is our freedom to choose our way and build our own life. Each person is a constant project: changing, adapting—sometimes for the better, other times for the worse. We wander our entire lives to find better places to live and better jobs, to learn new skills, to discover or invent something worthwhile. A prominent Bulgarian writer, Nikolay Raynov, has said:

> "A person is neither good fallen, nor proudly standing.
> He is beautiful when he is rising.
> Of all the scars in the footsteps of the road I liked only
> The wandering steps."

Love is natural; hate is learned. A child hugs and kisses another person long before he learns to hit and hurt. Yet as we grow, we become aware of all the hatred that fills this world—hatred toward those we know little to nothing about, simply because they have different beliefs, religions, skin color, or any other aspect that makes them not similar to us. What makes this book remarkable is that it shows people that, at our roots, we are all the same. What makes us different is due to where we grew up, what we were taught. No single rule fits all about how someone should live his life. Understanding diversity makes us stronger, smarter, more caring. Through various anecdotes, this book will show not only the pain that this lack of understanding has caused, but also the joy that embracing diversity and one's cultural heritage can bring.

In this book, I reflect upon my life abroad over the last twenty years as a Bulgarian immigrant. Through life stories and my canvas, I depict how traditions and rituals influence the formation of Bulgarian institutions and communities abroad. Culture is the temple for the soul; these communities help preserve the Bulgarian value system and beliefs. The book also shows the sorrow and the joy in the life of immigrants who are nostalgic for their native land, while at the same time trying to adopt and embrace their new life and surroundings. They want to be accepted and seen as equally valuable citizens in the new, adopted country.

One of the pillars for our success is our faith. Faith has preserved Bulgarians through the ages, and it continues to provide moral support even today for generations living outside our native country.

I don't like the word "immigrants." I think of people who are searching for a better life as "travelers" or "explorers." The world evolves and changes because people travel in search of new opportunities to better themselves, apply their ideas, or just for easier living. We are not immigrants; we are discoverers following our longing to explore a new world and more opportunities.

The word "immigrants" is a label created to divide people and foster hatred. In a world without borders, we all are citizens of Earth. Humans are projects; they constantly develop themselves as they search for a better life or new opportunities.

Would you call the English and the Spanish who first inhabited America immigrants? Probably not. Neither would you call the Proto-Bulgarian Khan Asparuh and his warriors immigrants. In 681, he led his tribe in search of water and land, and they founded present-day Bulgaria. Thracians inhabited those lands before Slavs claimed them. Customs and myths from both cultures are preserved in the Bulgarian lifestyle.

Nowadays, technology has removed borders. We wander not only by traveling to different places around the world, but also we travel in virtual space—either alone or with our families. We create new homes, find friends, raise our children, perform weddings, and say our farewells to friends and loved ones as we send them to the afterlife. Even thousands of miles from where we were brought up, we continue to observe and practice our customs. We share them with new friends who have a different heritage and faith, and we adopt new ones. We honor other cultures as much as we support people from our own community.

Many Bulgarians fled the country in 1989 after the change in the regime when Bulgaria became a democracy. The borders opened and the dreamers followed their vision—some to make more money or realize a dream, others to study or out of curiosity to find out about the "forbidden" world. Before the change, only a few were chosen to travel abroad—and then only to selected countries like the Soviet Union and the rest of the Socialist camp.

The West was hidden behind an iron curtain, and we were told only things our government wanted us to know. Not only traveling, but contact with the West was forbidden. My family had friends from West Germany, with whom they exchanged letters and pictures. In one of the letters, their daughter Veronica was holding a small tiger cub. I was so jealous and impressed that she could have a tiger cub as a pet. I couldn't imagine what else she might have. This was from the eyes of a nine-year-old girl. For us, the West was the Garden of Eden.

Later, when my brother had to go into the army, my family was told to stop our correspondence with this family. To punish us, they sent my brother to serve in one of the hardest regions in the country, as some called it, the Triangle of Death.

This wasn't the only reason they sent him there. In addition, we had a close relative who was an anticommunist and was serving time in the Belene camp. I didn't know him, but everyone in the family said his name with fear: "Uncle Vasil." We weren't partisans or part of the Communist regime; we were just a random family who worked hard and remained quiet generation after generation.

Even though one wall came down in 1989 and removed a curtain between the Eastern and Western worlds, today a new wall has been built, a wall of hate. After the changes in 1989, we were young enough to believe we could pursue our careers, support change, and build up our country from scratch. But something went wrong. Instead of moving forward, the country started to move backward. The leaders pointed fingers; they wanted to look at the archives, searching for former Communists, instead of moving the country onto the path of prosperity. While the government was busy implementing miserable ideas, in the background, the former Communist elite were building their underworld web, like a spider, sucking the blood and lifeforce from the country. I was working for a bank and had an opportunity to witness the bad and the good. I saw how many people were losing their homes and money, while others were building palaces from bones, violence, and fear.

Since I have a passion for art, in 1990, I traveled to Russia because Moscow had a lot to offer. But since they were part of the same camp, I didn't see a huge difference in lifestyle. I think Bulgaria was in an even better economic situation at the time. In Moscow, a bouquet of roses cost almost a month's salary. A few people there asked if I had goods from Bulgaria to sell. The most asked-for item was Bulgarian brandy, "Pliska." I was impressed by the people in Moscow; they were polite, but silent and sad.

Another trip that opened my eyes was to North Korea in the early nineties. Even today, I'm not sure if it was real or just a bad dream. I still have an image in my mind of the lines of people waiting to get a light bulb, something you could buy every day in Bulgaria. The trucks looked like ghosts from the 1940s, without windows and a faded green color. And fear was on people's faces when they talked about their lives. I've told my children that people there didn't have TV or if they did, they had one channel, which was on from 5 to 6 at night and carried only the local news. The people lived under a glass dome, and the only information they received was controlled by the government. And who knows if what they heard was fake or real news. It was heartbreaking to look at the people who were starving while they stood beneath the huge statue of their leader, bigger than the pyramids in Egypt. I felt relieved and secure only once I was on the plane ready to leave, with my passport in my pocket. After this trip, I appreciated what we had in Bulgaria.

This is why it's even more important to learn about other cultures, countries, and faith and appreciate our differences. Diversity is a fact; inclusion is a choice.

After 1989, I also visited Italy a few times, hoping to find a job and follow my passion for art. Italy was inspiring, but something was missing, not only the man I loved, but also my love for my country. I decided to go back to Bulgaria and give her a second chance.

My husband and I had ideas, money to invest, and energy. With a lot of effort and patience, we started a business. It was a constant fight for survival. We had to pay racket money to the local mafia and other groups and organizations in the chain. At the end, we didn't have enough money to grow our business. People who didn't want to pay or obey the rules lost parts of their body, some their lives. It wasn't just us, all small-business owners at the time were fighting the same battle. One day, I told my husband I didn't think Bulgaria was on the right path, and we needed to do something. He wasn't fond of my idea, but we, like many others who had lost hope, decided to leave our families and relatives and start a new life abroad.

As we like to say about that time, there wasn't any light in the tunnel. Fortunately, we were able to apply for the "Green Card" program and were approved. We sold everything and left the country. In the fall of the late nineties, I found myself and my family in New England.

Moving to America was a huge step. To make sure we didn't change our minds, we purchased one-way tickets. There is joy and sorrow moving to a new world, where you strive to preserve your identity, while at the same time attempt to adopt and assimilate the new culture and values in order to be accepted by society. Throughout the process, we also adopt new traditions and create new rituals. Many times in the beginning, I cried and was ready to pack and go back, but I stayed.

It was hard, not only because I missed my mom, brother, and relatives, but because I needed to learn a new culture and language and prove myself again. We experienced many rough friendships here; we lost friends and gained new ones. The pillar that helped us through these years was the Bulgarian community. Don't get me wrong; local people were helpful as well. But the real moral and spiritual support we gained was from the community.

Another thing that kept me moving was my faith and Bulgarian traditions. Traditions, faith, language, folklore, music, and dance are key elements uniting Bulgarians abroad. In our new country, Bulgarian rituals and folklore still have the main components that have been preserved for generations. We gather, we dance, we sing, and we eat and talk. We still pay respect to bread; it's the center of each celebration. Every time I felt rootless, I returned to my faith and my culture, reminding myself about the values that helped Bulgarians survive until today.

Traditions are a great way to teach children about the family's cultural and religious history, giving them personal identity. Customs, traditions, and beliefs give people hope for a better life for themselves and their families and friends. To understand other cultures, you need to learn about your own first. Knowing the effect of your culture will help you feel comfortable talking about your experiences, then you'll become better at listening to others talk about their culture. The term "culture" is not just about region or nationality. Even if we don't know who our ancestors are, we have culture.

In addition to the cultural groups we are part of, we also each have groups we identify with, such as being a parent, an immigrant, disabled, and so on. Being a part of such groups may be an identity that influences how you view the world and how the world views you. Becoming aware of your different identities can help you understand what it might be like to belong to a cultural group and accept other people's differences.

Many people support the idea that communities outside Bulgaria are formed and united by nostalgia. It's not nostalgia that unites them. Communities are built on common beliefs, worldviews, and values. Even when people go to a networking event, study in college, or meet up with friends at a party, they gather in groups in which everyone has something in common that unites them. We search for people who look like us, or like what we like. It may be that they share a belief, based on gender or political understandings. This is what communities are based upon, not nostalgia.

The feeling of nostalgia does exist within communities, however, because you can't erase your childhood and memories about home. Perhaps new generations born and raised abroad, outside Bulgaria, will be able to adapt to the new culture more easily.

Then the question arises: Should people who move to another country forget about their heritage and immerse themselves in their new culture? Should our children know about their heritage? Or should they retain the purity of their traditions, ignoring all else? Or perhaps a bit of both—creating new traditions from each culture?

There's no set answer. Everyone is different. What works for one person or family may not be appropriate for another. Some beliefs may be so strongly ingrained into people's personalities that no amount of time can erase them. Other beliefs may pass by the wayside, with people openly embracing new ones, or incorporating them into what they believe and creating new traditions.

Culture provides comfort and security. Customs, traditions, and beliefs give people hope for a better life for themselves and their children. Traditions are a great way to teach children about the family's cultural and religious history, giving them personal identity and roots. I encourage my family to learn new traditions from their friends, and to share our traditions with others.

Since the majority of Bulgarians are Orthodox Christians, many of us celebrate Easter twice—once on our own holiday, and again to honor friends and new relatives with different backgrounds, or just to make our children part of the surrounding culture.

What about marriages between Bulgarians and people of other ancestry? Will they cause problems when it comes to deciding what traditions to embrace? I've attended such weddings a few times, and I was pleased to see both sides desiring to learn something about each culture, respecting each other. Time will help overcome these differences. Every culture has something worthwhile; we need to get to know the beliefs and customs to appreciate them.

It's important to connect generations and keep the links alive. Spending time with older generations is a great way to build memories and enables people to learn about beliefs, traditions, and heritage. I'll leave you with a quote from my book *Mystical Emona: Soul's Journey* where Peter (a resident of a village in Bulgaria) is telling Stefan (a man who moved to the village from Boston) about Sultana (a *znahar*, a woman who heals with herbs), whom many people considered a witch: "When people don't understand things, they call them bad. Miracles still happen, but you need to believe deep in your heart before you can experience them."

So, culture is about believing. Culture is a temple for the human soul. It's something we take with us when we wander, and something we develop as we adapt to whatever place we call home.

The joy and the pain born from the words that follow, these stories and reflections, it was—and it is—my life. We get so worked up about things that we forget to see life. We all know how to love. It's natural. Let's help others to learn how to appreciate our differences and accept us no matter what our faith, color, or nationality.

Chapter 1: Faith

For centuries, faith has preserved the Bulgarian—from the oppressive rule of the Ottoman empire to the Communist regime in more recent times. Under Communism, the Church was represented as the enemy of ideology, and people were forbidden to confess their faith. But even during those years, the light of the candle and belief in God did not leave the Bulgarians. In every village in the most prominent place perched a white church. Like a lighthouse, it illuminated the road of life and guided people into the sea of the unknown—even as it still does today.

The most famous and honored person in villages was a priest. He baptized children in fear and secrecy, he married adults who swore their love for one another until death would separate them, and he finally completed the cycle of life by sending the deceased onto their eternal journey to the hereafter. In the church is also where children and women hid from the swords of the enslavers and thus survived to become a nation that is now scattered all over the world.

For those living abroad, the church plays a large role in the unification of Bulgarian communities and the preservation of our spirit and faith. In difficult times, we turn to faith and seek comfort for the soul, as well as support to continue our journey and face obstacles in life. It is abroad, far away from our parents and relatives, that religion is the connecting link that brings us together.

The role of the church for Bulgarians abroad is slightly different from its role in Bulgaria. In the beginning, the church was a community center. Everything revolved around the church and the school. This is not a surprise; we've been raised to believe and honor God.

Twenty years ago, a group of random teachers and parents in New England—brought together by our faith—established a school and a Bulgarian church to support the development of our children's sense of national identity. It doesn't have its own building and through the years has moved from one location to another, but still it keeps the candle alive and maintains the spirit of the Bulgarian faith and alphabet. For twenty years, volunteers have been making time from their busy schedules to teach or help in any way they can. Kindergartners learn how to make *martenitsi* (red and white amulets) or simply how to draw and color the letters of the Bulgarian alphabet. Children of all grades learn bits and pieces about Bulgarian history and culture.

A few years ago, I visited Chicago, where the biggest Bulgarian community in North America lives. It's like a little Bulgaria. There are soccer clubs, restaurants serving Bulgarian cuisine, a few newspapers in Bulgarian, and a Bulgarian TV station. I visited a church named after St. John of Rila. It's not surprising that the church is not only a religious place, but also an important social center devoted to maintaining language and tradition through Sunday schools and social gatherings.

Another beacon spreading light is the Bulgarian center Magura, a place to read, dance the *horo* (circle dance), or simply be part of an exciting event to meet people from the community. The visit was personal to me; it was the first audience where I shared one of my books, *Light Love Rituals: Bulgarian Myths, Legends, and Folklore*. I also shared the idea behind why I wrote the book: it was my way of keeping Bulgarian traditions and rituals alive for future generations.

In New England and other places abroad, even these institutions don't have a permanent home. Many are managed by volunteers, who strive to find ways to make the organizations survive so they can continue to gather young and old together for holidays and festivals. For many years, each small community has been holding events and raising money to build its own temple and a place to host the school and cultural events.

Why is it so important for these groups to have a home? Because the buildings themselves are a testament to the depths of the people's faith; building, preserving, and restoring churches is a way to convey one's beliefs. For Bulgarians, monasteries and churches have a special place in history and in our lives. The church is not only a temple of belief, but also a guardian of speech and traditions. For centuries, Bulgarian monasteries and temples have been cultural centers where they have given birth to some of the great relics of Bulgarian literature.

Throughout the centuries, monks have preserved more than religious beliefs; they have built and retained a nation's culture. For many, Italy is a place to visit. They go to see Venice's canal. Or, they may prefer to view the Leaning Tower of Pisa and have a bite of Italian pizza along with a glass of Chianti.

For me, it's also a place where I can pay respect to St. Cyril, one of the holy brothers who created the Glagolitic alphabet. His tomb is underground in the catacombs in Rome's San Clemente Basilica. It's hard to describe the feeling while I was there, staring at the centuries-old wall and the image of St. Cyril. Freshly cut flowers had been placed on the table. I learned from the tour guide that nuns from the nearby monastery bring flowers daily and keep them fresh.

St. Cyril and his brother, Methodius, used their alphabet in the year 863 to begin transcribing the Bible into Old Church Slavonic. From this script came the Cyrillic alphabet, which we use today. The two holy brothers are important not only to Bulgarians, but to all Slavs. They created a national identity through the use of letters and language, which are important to record and treasure history and culture. A unified language is also a way to share a nation's identity with future generations, so the information is not lost in the layers of time.

Another Bulgarian spiritual master was Chernorizets Hrabar. It's assumed this is not his real name; the words mean "brave person in a black shirt." Due to this name, everyone believes he was a monk. From 893 to 921, he wrote his one literary work, "On the Letters." In this book, he boasts of the superiority of the Glagolitic alphabet over Greek letters, which he said were neither the oldest known to the world, nor were they divine. He discusses the origins of the Glagolitic alphabet in the year 855, and how it could be improved, as well as talks about the Slavic Bible translation.

Another era that saw a revival of Bulgarian national spirit and socio-economic development occurred during the Ottoman occupation of Bulgaria, which lasted for nearly 500 years. This dark time ended with the country's liberation in 1878. During this time, faith and books were the pillars to keep the national spirit alive for half a millennium. The Bulgarian National Revival, also called the Bulgarian Renaissance, began in 1762, when Saint Paisius of Hilendar started writing his *Slavonic-Bulgarian History* (*Istoriya Slavyanobolgarskaya*). Within its pages, he describes the history of the Rila Monastery. About this holy place he says:

> "From all the Bulgarian glory, when so many monasteries and churches existed earlier in Bulgaria, in our time God left the Rila Monastery alone to exist all through the prayers of the holy Father John. It is a great benefit for all Bulgarians, so all Bulgarians are obliged to protect and give alms to the Holy Rila Monastery so that the great

Bulgarian benefit and praise they receive from the Rila Monastery through the prayers of our holy Father John, the glorious Bulgarian saint."

No wonder this place is called a Bulgarian treasure. The breathtaking monastery is nestled in the heart of the Rila Mountains. When you arrive, you're surrounded by the silence of nature. Wherever you look, you see a green carpet of pine trees, with the blue sky towering overhead. Every time I visit the monastery, I feel the spirit and the power of God. Even though I might be surrounded by tourists taking pictures and listening to their guide, for me, this sanctuary is not a tourist attraction, but a temple where I can re-energize my mind and purify my soul. It's hard to capture its beauty through the lens of a camera. It's an awesome experience listening to the cooing of the white doves sitting near the bell on one of the towers. When I look at the cold silhouette of the Hreliova Tower, one of the oldest buildings in the complex, I'm reminded about how it has been a place to hide treasure from attackers.

But the monastery is only one part of my visit here. My final destination is the St. John from Rila holy cave, a place where he spent seven years of his life in prayer. It's outside of the monastery in the mountain where you visit not as a tourist, but as a pilgrim to purify and connect to his holy spirit.

To enter the cave, you walk along a narrow path by a small church. According to legend, it was built by the first Rila Monastery monks. After you pass the church, your spiritual journey begins as you climb a few stone steps. In minutes, you enter into a dark, small hole. You crane your neck, attempting to see the ray of light at the top that's like a shower of hope and a blessing from God.

After you pass this test, you proceed to the *aizmo* (holy water at a nearby church). It's a place where you can drink cold, holy water from the spring. People believe that this water has healing power. Touching the purifying liquid, you can feel it dissolve in your body. When I wash my face there, I feel like a newborn. According to the local people, the water never freezes, even in the cold, winter months.

Near Rila Monastery is another inspiring place, a town called Melnik. Although one of the smallest towns in Bulgaria, it has seventy-five churches. Every time I visit Bulgaria, I go there to seek spiritual help and regenerate my being. It's not surprising that in the past this town was called the Bulgarian Mecca. Even today, while you walk between the ruins and the ivy-covered walls and broken marble slabs, you can feel the power of faith around you.

Early morning on one of my more memorable visits there, my family and I, along with a friend, were getting ready to leave the hotel to start our tour. I was looking for a place to pray for the health of another dear friend who was with me in spirit only. Most of the churches in Melnik are open for tourists to visit, so it's hard to find a quiet place for a spiritual connection. While I was asking our guide about such a place, a man in black who was passing by stopped. He offered to take me and my friend to a church where we could light a candle and pray. We accepted his offer and followed him down the stone-covered street, passing along a narrow, uphill path, until I finally saw a small church.

To my surprise, we didn't go to the main entrance, but went out back where there was a small, wooden door, half the size of the main doors. He turned around and gave me the metal key. It was heavy, dark, and rusted.

"You can open the door," he told me.

With trembling hands, I slid the key into the opening, turned it, and opened the door. My friend and the man entered the church before me.

"Welcome to St. Anthony Church," the man said. "I'll let you light a candle and pray. Don't rush. It's your home, God's home."

The church was small, preserved from the eyes and noise of tourists. I could smell the incense. The patina covering the icons had been preserved, never retouched, cleaned, or restored. A column stood in the middle of the space. At the bottom, I felt eyes on me; it was the icon of St. Anthony.

I don't know how long we stayed. Time felt as if it had stopped. When we finally got ready to leave, I thanked the man, and my friend and I returned to the hotel in silence. The power of that moment has remained with me until today.

Another cloister in which I've walked as a child with my grandmothers—and also with my children to introduce them to the Orthodox faith—is the Cherepish Monastery. It's near the village where I spent a lot of my time during the summer. In the village, as everywhere in Bulgaria at that time, religion was forbidden. But even during these times, every year on August 15, the Assumption of Mary, everyone in the village wore new clothes, and women gathered roses and *zdravets* (Bulgarian geraniums) from the garden. They baked bread from the whitest flour and roasted lambs or roosters.

By car or bus, villagers go to the monastery, along with hundreds of other people from around the region and throughout Bulgaria. They visit to worship Mary, God's mother, to pray for health, and to purify their souls. My favorite part as a child was the picnic at the end where everyone shared a meal and a story.

The monastery hasn't always been so tranquil. During a Turkish invasion, it was burnt and later restored by the locals. According to legends, the name of the monastery comes from the white color of the bones of Bulgarian soldiers who perished in battles with Ottoman raiders. Carved in the rocks there is a small building called "Kostnitza" (bone holder). If you climb up and enter the room, you can see an altar and also a place filled with human bones behind a glass wall. This is a reminder about those who lost their lives to preserve the freedom of our people.

One of my favorite memories when visiting churches was in the summer of 1998. I stood under the dome of the ruined church in Emona on the coast of the Black Sea. The wind danced inside the church and blasted the cracked walls, which were covered with faded paintings. I felt the gaze of the cracked faces of the icons painted by the hands of talented, unknown artists centuries ago.

The light shone through the window in the form of a rudder and lit the altar. The church was ruined, but I felt the joy of many baptisms, weddings, and rituals held there throughout the years. I could imagine the thundering of the Thracian legions and their giant horses as they galloped with pride as portrayed in *The Iliad*. I heard the cry of the baby who was just baptized and the music of the *tupan* (drum) and *kaval* (shepherd's pipe) celebrating the union of two souls. I envisioned a woman and man dressed in colorful costumes and flowers. I imagined kids holding baskets with Easter eggs. On their wrists dangled bracelets woven from white and red strings, a sign for happiness and good health.

The whirlwind of galloping horses that run wild in Emona brought me back to reality, but the moment remained imprinted on my mind. It inspired me to write my debut novel, *Mystical Emona: Soul's Journey*. A quote from the book sums up not only my feelings about that moment, but also the spirit of Bulgarians and their faith:

> "The church was several centuries old. It had been destroyed and rebuilt time and again over many generations. It had seen many weddings and christenings

and had housed countless people during disaster and wars. Although it was old and battered, it always restored his [Stefan's] energy and cleansed his soul."

In the same way, it cleansed my soul.

Chapter 2: Bulgarian Magical Wand

The day after Thanksgiving, snowflakes drift from the sky, swirling in a wintry dance. A frosty bite clings to the air as my family and I bundle up on our way to get a freshly cut Christmas tree from a nearby farm. We've been going there for the last twenty years.

All around us, children laugh as they hide among the branches. Our two girls are now grown, so they no longer join in the fun. Families walk around, inspecting and poking each tree to find the perfect one. We make our way around, doing the same. I breathe in deep, enjoying the pine-forest scent that makes this annual event special and joyful. After inspecting ten to fifteen trees, we find the perfect one.

Like everyone else on our street, and in our neighborhood and town, we are preparing for Christmas. We started this tree-picking tradition after we arrived in America. It was late fall, and the days were getting darker. We had plenty to occupy our time as we built our new life: we had to find a new home, get a school for the kids, and find jobs. I needed something to lift my spirit.

One of the first things we did when we moved to our apartment was to get a real tree. It was big, but it was special because it was part of a new tradition. That year we received a lot of presents from people we didn't know. Everyone was generous, welcoming us to the neighborhood. The hospitality, along with the light on our tree, made the dark winter speed by.

The tree this year was a little taller than normal, but I didn't argue. My children chose it, and it brought a smile to their faces. My husband is handy, so he cut the trunk to make sure we had space near the ceiling to place the angel. We set the tree in a reserved spot close to the fireplace and near the windows. On the wall behind the tree sits a mirror in the shape of the sun. I like it because when the tree is fully decorated, it looks like an oriole behind the angel.

Armed with a cup of hot cocoa, we gaze at the bare branches. Each year we have to decide who will put on the lights, because as usual they're tangled, and it takes time to remove the knots. Also, whoever's in charge of the lights needs to test them and make sure they're all working. Usually my husband teams up with one of the girls while the other helps with the ornaments.

Twenty years ago, we purchased a box of shiny, golden ornaments from Walgreens, but since then, our collection has become larger and more personal. Each year as part of the tree tradition, we purchase a new ornament for ourselves from places we visit together or neat little local shops, and we also get some from friends and teachers. I pick up one: a little red apple with a sign. It looks like it came from one of my youngest daughter's teachers back in 2001. A little reindeer with a red nose peeks out of the box. We created this as a school project. As I look through the box, each piece makes me smile with the memories behind the ornaments coming to life.

Covered with lights and with the last decoration added, the tree has come to life—golden and filled with memories. The angel on top looks over us, and I pray that she keeps us all safe and healthy and brings joy to everyone. My cat hides under the tree, waiting for the right moment to snatch a low-hanging decoration. I've learned my lesson from her past adventures, so now I place a few plastic objects near the bottom just for her. My dog is not with us this Christmas, so this casts a little shadow of gloom. We got him one past Christmas, and he spent many happy years near the tree. This Christmas, I made a special ornament for him, to make sure he remains with us in spirit.

Everything about the season is not as tranquil as the tree-decorating event. We get stressed as we run around looking for stocking stuffers and gift cards at the last minute. It's easy to waste two hours looking for a parking spot, never mind the time spent in crowded stores looking for the perfect presents. It's worth it, though, to see the smiles the gifts bring. But then over time, unfortunately, those gifts, lovingly chosen, become something the receiver ceases to enjoy. You wonder why.

Unnecessary things, and clothes we've forgotten that we have, overwhelm our lives. We shove them into the closet, and we don't even remember who gave them to us. The smiles they brought when we received them are long forgotten. Christmas wasn't always like this for me.

In Bulgaria, Christmas was forbidden. For more than forty-five years, Bulgaria was a Communist country, so it was inappropriate to celebrate religious holidays. Christmas day, like any other religious holiday in Bulgaria, was a working day. New Year's was the New Christmas or Koleda. Even though everyone could celebrate New Year's openly, most people, including my family and grandparents, would secretly perform the old Christmas traditions on that day.

We didn't have Santa Claus, but the identical Russian version called "Dad Moroz." He was a friendly looking old man with a long, white beard and a red suit. He gave presents to the children, but he didn't come down the chimney. He entered through the front door and met us in person. Most importantly, we received gifts on the evening of December 31 instead of on December 25.

Each year, I waited to get a doll I wanted to have for a long, long time, or a blouse I'd been looking at through a window shop for months. The presents were so meaningful to me that I was afraid to play with the doll. Sometimes, I kept it in the box for months. I'm sure my mother still has some of my dolls in her memory boxes. Even an orange was a great gift. New Year's celebrations were the only time people had the chance to taste what was then considered exotic fruits: bananas, oranges, tangerines, and others. These were impossible to find during the rest of the year.

The new year was a time of remembrance. And what better way to remember than through food and smells. Even though Bulgaria is a small country, its cuisine is diverse. The meals, like the colors woven into the nation's rugs, represent the hospitality and rich spirituality of its people. The food gathers people around the table where the many generations can talk and connect. Even my grandmother's cats waited quietly near the stove for a taste of the special holiday bread.

I learned most of the rituals, cooking, and traditions from my grandmother. Some I only observed, while others I helped her perform and prepare. Before dinner, she purified the house and bread with smoke from incense burning on hot coals. I walked behind her, wanting to carry the metal container holding the embers.

Once everything was ready, we sat around the table to eat and talk. On New Year's, the dinner table was similar to how the Christmas (Koleda) table would have been set. It held the traditional ritual bread with fortunes. We didn't have a fireplace in my grandmother's house, but she cooked and baked bread on a wood stove. Instead of only the customary vegetarian meals we'd normally have at Christmas, the New Year's table contained a variety of traditional meals including meat. My mother and grandmother prepared delicious dried red peppers filled with rice, spices, and sometimes boiled, crushed beans.

Even though it was forbidden for Bulgarians, Christmas was, and is, an important holiday. In the past, it reflected the beginning of the winter holidays. The harvest had been picked, the wine bottled, and the grain milled. Everyone was ready to rest and celebrate a quiet holiday. On Christmas Eve, the family gathers around a special table and also respects the deceased predecessors of the home. It's a night full of magic and love.

Some of these traditions are preserved and practiced here (abroad) among our Bulgarian community. Families and friends gather to celebrate with meatless dishes and the famous soda bread (*pitka*) with lucky fortunes and a coin baked inside. Everyone prepares what they've learned from their grandmother, mother, or from information and recipes on the Internet. It's a world without borders, and we have access to all kinds of information to make our celebration unique for us. On Christmas, we also drink a homemade brandy called *rakia*.

Whoever fails to find the lucky coin has a second chance on New Year's Eve when a special pastry called *banitsa* is made. The hostess puts fortunes in the banitsa and makes sure each guest gets a piece with one. What is a banitsa? It's the queen of the Bulgarian cuisine and among other societies. It's an egg-and-cheese-filled pastry made from filo dough.

Nowadays, we make the traditions special by sharing with our neighbors. In return, they share specialties from their ancestry. Our Greek neighbor's baklava is famous in the neighborhood. She also makes a *spinakopita* (a Greek banitsa), which I admit is quite tasty. We also know an Italian family who prepares food for the whole street, plenty of wine and a variety of dishes.

The Italians also prepare and serve a special multi-course seafood dinner on Christmas Eve (La Vigilia). It's a wonderful holiday mealtime tradition that originated in Southern Italy and is known as the Feast of the Seven Fishes. They make bread and have adopted our "fortune coin" tradition.

After the Christmas fever passes, we count the days to New Year's. As we say in Bulgarian, "New year, new luck." Since for most of my life, New Year's was the New Christmas, I can't watch a movie and eat Chinese takeout quietly at home. It's still an important day for my family and friends. We usually gather in a friend's house or in a lake cabin and prepare a variety of food in Bulgarian style. We cook and clean for two days, bake bread, and make banitsa with fortunes.

As the New Year rings in, our energy levels are high. We make a toast with sparkling champagne and dance the Danube horo, while we eagerly await the arrival of the Survakari. If you ask my children, I'm sure they'll say this is a weird ritual. Survakane nowadays are the youngest members of the family, the children. We teach them how to sing and perform the ritual. They chant "Surva, Surva Godina" while patting every guest on the shoulder with a *survachka* for health and prosperity in the New Year. To make sure you receive their luck, you have to give money to the singers.

Survachki are made from dogwood because it's the healthiest tree. It's adorned with yarn, wool, popcorn, dried fruit, beads, and other small items. Each survachka is unique. I used to teach in the Bulgarian school years ago, and I demonstrated to kids how they can make them. It's a fun activity to learn about your Bulgarian heritage. I call it a magic wand. The survachka has an ancient story. The stick held power to chase away evil spirits, which, during the winter solstice, could cross the threshold between the spirit world to the land of the living.

We don't have dogwood here, so we improvise. If we find a fruit tree, that's fine, but when no tree is appropriate, the idea is to continue the tradition of the magic wand. Making the survachka is an opportunity for old and young to be together and to create something they'll remember and pass on to their children.

Cheers, "Nazdrave," and a prosperous year! Fill your homes with health, children, and abundance.

Chapter 3: Wine and Love

My husband and I built our lives and raised our children in the same house for more than twenty years. When we moved there, one of our first projects was to build an *asma*, a wooden or metal structure like a pergola to support a climbing grapevine. In Bulgaria, they form a cover or tunnel over a garden patio.

The grapevines on the asma grew along with our children, getting stronger and bigger with each passing year, creating a lavish green cover over the patio and fish pond. During all that time, we gathered under the shadow of the leaves around the round table to celebrate birthdays, friendship, and life. In the spring, I collect fresh leaves and stuff them with rice and meat. I call them "Bulgarian sushi." They're a traditional meal in the Balkans and in the Middle East. In the warm days of summer, the asma has been a place to sit and relax. In the fall, the grapes attract birds and bees, and we share the sweet fruit with them.

Whenever you go to a Bulgarian house here, you'll find a grapevine and a vegetable garden. The gardens are small, but you'll be amazed at the variety they produce. Bulgarians are well-known gardeners, and this is true here as well. In some gardens, you can find nettle and other rare, exciting varieties known for their curative power. Another plant that is famous and beloved is the Bulgarian geranium called zdravets, an herb spoken about for centuries in songs and poems.

Let me explain why the asma and grapevines are so important to us. The asma is where friendship is offered around the table or just a place to take a break from work to sit in the shade. Under the grapevine and in the vineyard are where we celebrate wine and love every year on February 14. This day is not only St. Valentine's Day, it's also Trifonovden, St. Trifon's Day, one noted for festivities surrounding grapes and wine.

Wine has an important place in the life of Bulgarians. Each region in Bulgaria is known for a specific type of wine, and they all have their unique tastes and quality. Bulgaria was one of the largest wine producers, but lost its place after the government changes in 1989. The glory of Bulgarian wine has been written about around the world and has been raved about by many connoisseurs of fine wines.

Based on historical facts, Winston Churchill was one of those known connoisseurs. Every year, he ordered wine from Melnik, a small town in Bulgaria famous for its red wines. The climate and soil produce heavy, full-bodied wine with a unique taste. In the town, which has no more than 300 inhabitants, there is a wine museum, and almost every house has a cellar carved into the rocks where the sparkling red liquid is stored. The mastery of making wine is passed from generation to generation.

Like everyone in rural Bulgaria, my grandparents produced wine. My mother still keeps this tradition alive in her small vineyard. It's a ritual she performs the entire year, starting with paying respect to the god of wine in February. After months of hard work, she harvests the grapes in late fall when they've turned into red, holy juice and puts it into wooden barrels that have been in use for many generations. An important part of the process is to clean the barrels with warm water and other special ingredients inside and out to make sure everything is clean, pristine, and ready for the young wine. She also puts a cotton bag containing herbs into the barrels to make the taste of the wine unique and bring out its healing power. Each household has their own recipe. One popular ingredient is St. John's Wort, an herb used by healers.

Before 1941, my paternal grandparents owned a small inn, called a *khan*. It was established in the nineteenth century by our great-grandfather Zarko. It was at the center of the village Luti Dol on the main road to Sofia. There were many legends about famous people stopping by, including one about the Bulgarian Apostol Levski, one of the most-loved heroes, who was called the "Apostle of Freedom." During the last two wars, many women and children hid in the cellar to survive the occupation. The Communists had many reasons to keep our family on their blacklist.

I still remember the buildings; it was a small complex. Each building had a well-built foundation and construction. The wooden columns were similar to ones you'd see in monasteries, carved from the trunks of pine trees and colored by the patina of time.

When you passed through the two wooden gates, the main house was on the left. It was built in the late 1700s; its roof was covered with black stone tiles covered with moss, typical for Bulgarian houses and monasteries. In the main house, travelers would find the kitchen, a bigger room used as a place to drink and eat, and a barber shop. My grandfather was the barber and also the cook. His soups still bring back fond memories. My grandmother helped him cook and serve the food, wine, and other drinks. She was a good baker. I still can taste the warm bread baked in the *podnitza* (a round earthen dish) set on coals in the hearth on the covered porch. My favorite was her banitsa, made from homemade filo dough, butter, and feta cheese.

To the right of the gates was a small garden with a grapevine asma, with berry bushes, herbs, and a well in the middle. We didn't use the well, because someone had thrown a dead animal there after the revolution in 1944. The well was covered with wooden planks, and all of the kids were forbidden to go near it. My grandmother told us that a *talasum* lived in the well. Thoughts about this terrifying spirit, created by burying a person or animal into a wall to act as a protector of a place, were enough to keep us away.

The yard was filled with ducks and chickens. On the right was a place where travelers used to park their carriages and feed their horses and donkeys. After 1944, during the nationalization, this was turned into a place for villagers to keep their sheep and other animals. It wasn't convenient, but my grandparents didn't have a choice but to obey the rulers and give their house to the government. It was sad to see my grandparents hiding in one of the rooms in their own house.

Also to the right of the gate was a more modern, two-story white building, which held five or six guest rooms. Stairs on the outside led to the second floor which had a long terrace covered with terracotta. After 1944, the new regime took over the building and left only one room for my grandmother to live in. She didn't have a pension, so she collected herbs, mushrooms, and snails to sell to make money. She lost everything, but never lost her spirit, even up until she died at the age of ninety-nine.

After 1989, we didn't get the inn back because the Communists destroyed the building. This was sad not only because it belonged to my family, but because the old khan held a lot of history. My grandmother told me my great-grandfather had bought it from a monastery at an auction. He was a wise man. During the auction, the deal was when a lit candle went out, whoever made the last bid would get the building. My great-grandfather bid only one lev (Bulgarian money) every time it was his turn, and he finally won the building.

After the government took over, since the hotel wasn't functioning, government officials turned most of the rooms into a warehouse. One room was filled with tobacco leaves, another with herbs. Others held old radios, beds, empty bottles, glasses, and plates.

We use to play hide-and-seek with my cousins in these rooms, wandering around, searching for unusual treasure. One of our discoveries was an old Philips radio. It was functioning but was stuck on one station. On the back we discovered the tuner string had been blocked with a red wax stamp, which prevented us from moving the dial from one station to another. We were kids, so we didn't understand a lot about what we could listen to and what we could say at the time.

Some of the former guest rooms had been turned into a workshop for making plastic bottles. I still remember the smell of burning plastic and the little white and green beads spilled all over the yard and the terrace. The pay was good in the shop, but my grandmother wasn't allowed to work there. To survive, she gathered herbs and blackberries, and worked for other people in their fields and vineyards. She kept her pride her entire life. Even when the house was filled with strangers, she was able to keep up her spirit, cook and bake, tell us stories about our family, and celebrate everyday life. One thing I remembered from her was the saying "Better to be in the people's mouth, not in their feet."

The most remarkable part of the property after the hearth was an old pear tree, offering a cool shade in the summer and juicy fruit in the fall. Near the tree was the entrance to the cellar. At least this space was preserved and was used only by my family, but not to the same extent as when the hotel was functioning and they had guests. It was a place to remember: always cold and dark, it smelled like a mix of wine and mold, and I could feel the dampness. The barrels were different sizes. Ten to fifteen people could easily fit into the two at the bottom. I don't think this was my childhood imagination; they were huge. They remained empty since 1944, but were a reminder of the old times.

My grandmother was poor and she used wine, honey, and herbs to cure coughs and everything else. She mixed wine and black pepper, wine and honey, and boiled wine with different herbs. My grandfather drank the wine and the rakia produced from the wine to heal his soul and forget what was stolen from him until he left this world early.

The building was destroyed in the 1980s, and now the place is covered with ivy and weeds, a reminder of the Communist era. The day they demolished the building, we lost a trace of my family, my grandparents, and memories. My grandfather spent most of his life trying to save his home by going from one place to another. He walked to the courthouse with a leather folder like a briefcase filled with documents.

When the village was established in 1428, fifteen families lived there. My relatives are from an old family called Zarkovtzi. After the plague in 1830, families from other villages moved there. In the 1930s, the village had over 1,300 residents, but now it's slowly dying like many other villages in Bulgaria. Mostly older people live there now, or newcomers searching for tranquility and purity in nature. They keep the spirit alive by performing rituals and celebrating holidays, weddings, and name days.

An old picture in the post office shows the village center and my grandparent's inn. I have a more recent picture, but the place where my grandparents' house was is now empty, a legacy lost. If I don't capture the history, nobody will know about the house that was there for centuries, a house that witnessed the Ottoman, German, and Russian occupations and many more historical moments.

It's no wonder why wine is so important to Bulgarians. It has an old history going back to the Thracians, who used to live in the area which is now modern Bulgaria, Greece, Turkey, and at one time even extended farther. Thracians were fine craftsmen; they believed in immortality and had beautiful horses. Some scholars speculate that when the Thracians populated the area, they were the first to bring viticulture to the region. They brought grape vines, cultivated them, and began wine production.

In the past, Trifon Zarezan was a popular event in February. Groups of men, young and old, went to the nearby vineyards, bringing food and wine to celebrate the day. After setting their bags of food, *baklitsi* (wooden vessels for wine), and tools down, they walked around the outside of the vineyard, holding up icons of Saint Trifon. When they returned to the starting point, they faced east and made the sign of the cross three times. The oldest in the group would kneel by a strong grapevine root and pour red wine around it three times. He also broke a crust of bread and put four pieces into the hole, equal distances apart, saying, "How many drops in the wine that many grapes in the vineyard this year."

They also scattered "magical" ashes around the vines to ensure a good harvest. The ashes came from a *budnik*, a log burned on Budni vecher, Christmas Eve. Sometimes a priest went to the vineyard, but since he was old, I don't remember seeing him as part of the festivities. In some villages, people also selected a "King of the vineyard." His success during the year ensured everyone else would have bountiful harvests.

They used shoots from the grapevine to make a wreath to decorate their baklitsa or to wear as crowns. They'd also cut more shoots to take home to place by the family's icons. My grandmother kept the wreath and used it in the fall when she made sauerkraut. She placed it into a barrel to cover the cabbage and make sure the juice stayed steady and didn't get too sour. She also used the shoots in winter soups and other cooking recipes.

The February pruning rite was merely symbolic. The actual pruning occurred the following month. It was a simple celebration of the liquid, red gold, given to us by gods to cure sickness, bring us joy, and cheer us when we needed comfort.

No table lacks wine; it's part of weddings, name days, and bereavements. It's part of life. Nowadays, people continue to congregate in the vineyards, sing songs, and celebrate. The tradition has its own followers here as well. Whoever has a name day that day opens the doors of his home for relatives and friends. Wreaths are also made from vine rods, like the wreath of Dionysus.

The feast day is important for our family here as well. Each year, my husband cuts a small rod from the grape vine, and we drink a glass of wine. From the bottle, we sprinkle the liquid around the roots of the grapevines for prosperity and health. Normally in New England, the yard is covered with snow on this day, so you see the red dots over the snow. It looks like blood. We keep the tradition alive and perform the ritual every year. My husband grew up in Sofia, the capital of Bulgaria, and this tradition was unknown to him. But after we moved to the suburb, he adopted it, and this is a ritual we do together every year. It takes time to create new traditions in your family.

Of course, here February 14 is a double holiday. The feast merges with the holiday of love, Valentine's Day. Could anything be better than wine, chocolate, red roses, and the warmth of close friends? We also celebrate with a special appetizer called *lukanka*, which is similar to the Italian dry salami. I think Valentine's is every day when two people love each other.

We have a friend whose name day falls on Valentine's. We traditionally visit his home, bringing him a present and desserts. Usually this brings together a lot of people. We drink wine and dance till dawn. Yes, even if the feast is during the week, the party is done Bulgarian-style. Bulgarians work hard, but they also know how to celebrate and rejoice.

As one of my aunts says, "What more does a person need if they have wine and love?"

Chapter 4: Martenitsa – a Thread of Hope

Sometimes, we need a sign or a miracle to encourage and empower us. As Oprah Winfrey likes to say, "Life is whispering to us; we need to listen." It's important to understand the signs and follow our intuition.

Years ago, on a gloomy, rainy spring day, I was dragging my feet with a bowed head, absorbed in personal and work-related problems that stifled my soul. I was in Boston Public Garden; I didn't see or hear anything because I was so closed off inside my world. Anger tightened my throat, and my coat weighed me down like iron.

Then, in the distance, I saw a flower perched on the bare branches of a tree. It danced like a butterfly. When I came closer, I noticed that it wasn't a flower; it was the traditional Bulgarian amulet called martenitsa. I knew for certain because it wasn't any random martenitsa, but Pijo and Penda, the boy and the girl made with red and white threads.

For the people passing by, this amulet meant nothing. But for me, it was a ray of light penetrating the clouds. I felt that somewhere near me, someone shared my cultural beliefs. Someone had put the martenitsa on the branch hoping for health and good omens. People going by were walking their dogs, chatting, and taking pictures. I stopped to look at their faces, hoping to spot the person who might have put the amulet there. I was looking for a sign. Perhaps the person would come back and touch the martenitsa.

People smiled at me, and a group of cheerful girls stopped to touch the martenitsa, but they didn't know about it. They didn't even know where Bulgaria was, but I expected that. I proudly described what it meant and the history of the amulet. They looked puzzled. One of them said she thought it was the Kabala Amulet or a sacral ritual. They took some pictures and went back to their own world. A little birdie was singing its song at the top of the tree; I felt it was talking to me to cheer me up and help me embrace the day.

The wind blew away the clouds, and the sun bloomed over the branches covering them and the martenitsa with gold. A few sparkling drops of water trickled down from the branch onto my hair and face. I wiped my cheeks with my palm and felt refreshed from their cold touch. The sun shone and tickled my face. Although I wore several layers of winter clothes and held my laptop bag, I felt as light as a feather, ready to fly in the breeze. I left the garden, turned a few times and still saw the boy and the girl dancing on the branch.

On my way home on the train, I looked out the window and kept my eyes glued to the last sun rays. The day was gone, but I had hope that tomorrow would be better. The martenitsa for me was a sign, a sign to embrace the positive in anticipation of a new beginning from the universe. As Byron says, "O, wind, If winter comes can spring be far behind."

In Bulgarian folklore and traditions, the martenitsa is a symbol of the coming of spring and of new life and new beginnings. Several legends describe the origins of this amulet. I'll tell you one that's in my book *Light Love Rituals: Bulgarian Myths, Legends, and Folklore*. The tale is about Penda and Pijo, the girl and boy I found dancing in the wind.

Penda and Pijo

A long time ago, a Tsar named Pijo loved a woman named Penda. When Pijo found out she had been kidnapped, he wanted to search for her, but he couldn't leave his kingdom. He sent carrier pigeons with messages asking his loyal subjects if they'd seen Penda. He also asked a brave, trusted soldier to look for her. The man left on a hot summer day and searched for her well into winter.

Far from his homeland, he met an old woman and eleven old men sitting on the cold ground by a well. The old woman struggled to rise, so the soldier helped her, then lifted the bucket of water from the well to give her a drink.

She said, "I'm Baba Marta (Grandmother March), and these are my brothers, the other eleven months of the year. Because you've been kind to me, you'll find what you're looking for."

Soon the soldier discovered the house where Penda was held prisoner. He untied her and was going to take her home, when the man who kidnapped her returned. They fought for many hours. The soldier tired and feared his strength would fail. He jabbed once more and killed the bad man, then collapsed. Penda gave him a drink of water.

"Our journey back will take a long time," she said. "I must let Pijo know I'm safe." She wrote a note and placed it inside a tube. With a white thread, she tied it to the leg of a carrier pigeon Pijo had sent, then released the bird.

Along the way, the bird scraped its leg on a branch. Blood had stained the thread by the time the bird finally reached Pijo. When he read the note, he was so happy. He tied the blood-stained thread to his shirt until Penda returned safely.

That's one story about why we use red and white to make martenitsi even today.

When my family and I traveled to Bulgaria a few years ago, we visited a small village in the south called Zlatolist (Gold Leaf). My visit there wasn't accidental. I had heard a lot about this unique place as a powerful energy center and spiritual place and wanted to explore and learn more. Since it was near Melnik, everyone in my family agreed to do a day trip. In Zlatolist is where a beloved Bulgarian prophetess and healer, Reverend Stoyna (1883 – 1933), lived her life in a temple devoted to St. George. People from all over Bulgaria and Europe traveled to meet her and ask for her advice, for herbs, and for her to heal them. She is still alive in the local people's memories and stories about miracles she performed. Even Baba Vanga (1911 – 1996), who was a well-known prophetess, traveled to Zlatolist to gain energy and pray.

The road to the village was covered with mud and in bad shape from the water and the years. It reminded me of the road to Emona, which I've written about in my book *Mystical Emona: Soul's Journey*. I was afraid our car would break down, but finally we saw the golden cross and arrived at St. George's temple.

Silence. Omnipresent silence. I have no words to describe it

We entered through the gate. Behind the white wall, the yard was filled with green bushes and flowers on this June day. People were walking under the noon sun, and the temple was open for visits. Inside, the faces of the saints welcomed us to the holy place. A few people were paying respect and praying in front of the altar. Candles illuminated their faces, creating an amber glow. The wooden floor squeaked under my feet. In the middle of the temple under the dome is a marble slab with a carved double-headed eagle, the symbol of God or according to some people, the seal of the Bulgarian church. It's believed such a spot is marked by the church because it has high energy and healing power. Sick people remove their shoes to stand barefoot on the plate to absorb the energy into their body.

An older woman gave us a pamphlet and pointed to the end of the room where stairs led to the second floor. In silence, we climbed them. Bursts of colors and gifts surrounded us at the top: colorful rugs, flowers, and other gifts. Icons with Reverend Stoyna's face were arranged around the floor, painted by artists and random people. She had been blind, but looking at her face on one of the paintings, I felt as if she was piercing my soul. At the bottom of the main room was a small table and a notebook where people wrote their wishes.

"Go ahead. Write your wishes, child." An old grandmother in dark clothes handed me a pen.

I didn't want to disappoint her, so I bent over the paper. What could I wish for? Health. Health, happiness, and love for everyone. What else could I ask?

I stepped back and the person behind me bent over the notebook. She made the sign of the cross and started writing. I could see how her face changed; it was the look of hope. I left, giving her privacy, and went to explore.

On the right was Stoyna's room, where she spent her life in prayer and fasting. It was a small room, big enough to hold a bed. But what took away my breath was the ceiling covered with pictures. A universe of faces of girls, boys, and hundreds of eyes watching me from above. I heard the prayers of their mothers, fathers, the prayers for hope. My eyes filled with tears, and I ran away. It was too much to take in, too much pain.

I needed to get out. I needed air. Outside in the middle of the yard was a tree, but it wasn't an ordinary tree; it was a sycamore. I'd seen some before. This tree was as old as Bulgaria. Imagine if the tree could talk. I wonder how many tales we could learn. It's been there for over thirteen centuries.

Its branches were covered with martenitsi, and in its trunk it hid folded pieces of paper with wishes for health and prosperity. There's a legend that the tree can produce miracles, and everyone who stays under its crown or hugs the tree will heal. In the yard of the monastery, there's also a magical well. You just need to bend over the well and whisper your wish to the eternal water.

Miracles abound in the air in this holy place. Whether you believe or not, it's a place to visit and reflect. Reflect about your life, your loved ones, remind yourself what's important in life. The tranquility and purity around help reduce stress and recharge energy.

I went back to the tree, listening for its voice. I looked above my head. The green leaves mixed with the white and red of the martenitsi reminded me of a blanket, a temple of hope.

Our life is a journey filled with obstacles, joy, love, disappointments, and sickness. We need to climb; we need to rise if we have fallen. The hope in miracles and healing is what helps us keep moving. Creating a martenitsa is another way for us to believe, hoping the amulet will bring us health, love, and happiness.

In my family, March 1, Baba Marta Day, is one of our favorite holidays. We love to make martenitsi to give to friends and family. This ritual is preserved and spread across borders and abroad. Millions of Bulgarians carry the amulet with pride in the spring to welcome the new beginnings of life in nature. In Bulgaria, people tie their martenitsi to a tree when they see a stork, which signifies the arrival of spring. Since we don't have storks here, Blagovets, March 25, is the day we perform this ritual. We put the martenitsi on an apple tree in our garden and make wishes. When we moved into the house, we planted the tree. Now twenty years later, the tree is covered with red and white. This was my inspiration for one of my paintings called "Martenitsa."

In 2016, when I presented my book *Light Love Rituals* in Chicago, one of the Bulgarians told me a story about a tree trimmed with martenitsi in the Chicago zoo. The tree is in front of the stork cage, and this is where Bulgarians created a tradition to go and put their amulets every spring. On my way back to Boston, the idea of *The Miracle Stork* was born. It's a children's short story about faith and the power of the family.

The tradition is different now from what it was back in those days. Many of my friends who are of a different faith and nationality also wear a martenitsa. They adopted this tradition, and they eagerly await the first of March to receive a new one from me. For me, a martenitsa is an amulet for friendship, love, and hope.

Chapter 5: Flowers and Love

Laughter fills the house this Sunday. It's not an ordinary Sunday; it's Flower Day or Tsvetnitca (Palm Sunday, the week before Easter). Bulgarians love both the day and its rituals, which celebrate love, flowers, and the rebirth of nature. By Palm Sunday, spring has arrived. After the gray winter, everybody craves colors and the sun.

A waterfall of greenery covers the weeping willow in our yard. We traditionally make wreath belts by twisting together the branches, so our girls will be healthy, slender, and beautiful. Over the years as they've become adults, the ritual has lost its vivid nature and details. Now it's more symbolic. However, we still collect spring flowers and green willow branches and place them around the icon of Our Lady and around the entryway like a wreath.

Along with Palm Sunday, Lazar's Day (St. Lazarus' Day or Lazarovden, the day before Palm Sunday) is another of the most celebrated holidays. It's symbolic of health and longevity. When Jesus' friend Lazarus died and was buried, the Son of God shouted into the tomb, "Lazarus, get up," and the man rose from the dead.

Lazar's Day was once a day for marriage proposals. Unmarried girls eagerly waited for this important day. They dressed in their newest clothes, combed and braided their hair, gathered flowers, and made floral wreaths that they'd wear for Flower Day.

In the past, these *lazarki*, as the girls were called, went on a tour around the village, singing songs for health and prosperity. All the girls participated in the custom because it was believed that any girl who was not a lazarka couldn't get married. The girls were supposed to enter every house because it was a bad omen to miss one, and the family would have unhappiness. In return for visiting, the lazarki received gifts from the families.

Baba prepared a basket for the girls; it was filled with apples, walnuts, eggs, and onions and garlic braided together. We don't have lazarki here, but on the table we always have all the items my grandmother gave out in the past, plus honey and round, ritual pitka bread.

Some years a gypsy *katun* (a few families who traveled together from place to place) came to the village. I recognized them by their colorful carriages and the rattling of the copper vessels they carried. They went from house to house to collect old copper caldrons, pots, pans, and cookware. They used tin to cover the rust and make the inside of the items they collected like new to keep them safe to use. The young gypsies danced and told fortunes using beans, cards, or palm reading. In return, people gave them produce, household items, clothes, and fabric. If someone was wealthy, they might also give them a hen or chicken.

The katun stayed for a few days before they went to another village. From time to time, one of the villagers complained about missing hens or ducks, but they said that the fox or the hawk must have taken them away. They didn't blame the gypsies because they wanted to make sure the katun returned again the next year.

Back then, the village was filled with peace and tranquility, and everyone honored the other. Nowadays, the village has lost its spirit. People have become bullies, burning houses and attacking others with shovels, fighting over property.

Today, my family celebrates both Flower Day and St. Lazar's Day on Palm Sunday because everyone is busy on Saturday: sports games, weekly grocery shopping, driving the kids to volunteer at a shelter, and doing other family chores that prevent the family from gathering around the table. Instead, we eat on the go, and I drink my black coffee or iced green tea. Most of the time we get home after the sun has set.

Another tradition I love is that we Bulgarians honor the name of a person, and so we celebrate name days. For some people, they are even more important than their birthday. On Flower Day, we celebrate people whose names are flowers. I love to say that it's a feast for all women, because, for me, women are flowers.

One "flower" in particular was my Baba Tsvetana (called Tsenka for a nickname), my mother's mother, whose name means flower. We spent Palm Sunday with her. She always baked delicious bread and put on the table all the gifts of their labor and those from nature. She and my grandfather, Nikola, lived a simple life. They produced most of their food, didn't travel a lot, but they had their own world and this was enough for them to be satisfied. They raised their children, had a roof over their heads, and never stole or asked for donations. They built their lives working hard and were proud of what they had.

Baba was a Balkan woman who lost her mother when she was a child. By the time she became a young girl, she was given as a bride to my grandfather in an arranged marriage. When I was older, I asked her if she loved my grandfather. She said people learned to love, and love came with time.

I watched her with my grandfather, but I couldn't tell if it was love they shared or just a cohabitation agreement. They raised their children, cared for each other, and respected each other, spending their lives speaking good words to one another.

I couldn't spend time with them at their last hour because I was abroad, but I thought about them every day. I dedicate every Palm Sunday to my grandmother. From her, I learned to respect bread and people and appreciate the little things in life. When she was sad or had a lot on her mind, she told me a story or she sang to me. She also helped me relieve my pain when I was sick or sad and missing my parents. Baba liked to sing. My grandfather and I went out to the yard with her in the evening and sang under the starry sky while my eyes closed for sleep and the stars turned into fireflies.

On this current Palm Sunday, as I set the table for a festive lunch, I look at my daughters sitting next to each other, whispering their secrets. My beautiful flowers.

Like every mother I want my girls to be happy. Did I make mistakes while raising them? Did I share the lessons I learned through my life as Baba and my mother did with me? Will they find love and what they want in life?

For a moment, I return to my past, thinking about the girl I was who had dreams, the girl who believed in people, the girl with big hopes and ideas. I met a boy who promised to love me and care for me. At first, it was like those childhood sweetheart love stories. In most cases, they have a happy ending, but not for me. Jealousy overtook him, and he became abusive. My mind slips back to one memory....

I feel burning pain and the taste of iron in my mouth. Tears cover my eyes, and with a shaky voice, I barely answer his "I love you" with my own "And I love you." I swallow and feel his powerful hands squeezing my neck, the sting of his fist lingering on my burning cheek.

Is that love? To hurt someone and then pray for forgiveness and beg for their love. I want to run away, but the strongest always win, and I remain locked in an imaginary cage by his excuses and promises.

It's not always like this. Many times, we make plans, build towers of dreams, hold hands, and enjoy the little things. Suddenly, the bad guy returns to him again, jealous and tyrannical, thirsty for revenge and blood. I promise myself this will be the last time. My tears and his gifts won't block my way to freedom. I promise to love myself and get out of the cage woven by his empty promises and insults.

Pain like burning coals flows through my belly at the thought of leaving. I do love him, but this is the right step, the first step for me. Neither his hostile, threatening, uncaring phone calls nor his promises to change will stop me from leaving. The door behind me is closed; the fear remains locked away forever. Promises spoken and broken thousands of times, kisses scorched by insults, and fear of the next disgrace and offense are all gone.

I feel strange, like a slave who has been given his freedom. My love was poisoned. "I hate you, but I'll forgive you! I will forgive you, but never forget!" ...

"Mommy ... Mom ... see my wreath!" The bright face of my daughter returns me to the present and my world, the world of love. We arrange the table and decorate the ritual bread with flowers.

When you're hurt and deceived, it's hard to let another person touch your heart again. You hardly believe in tears and beautiful words.

But Fate often sends us gifts, gives us rewards for our suffering. And I received this gift, a gift of love. I met a man who loves me sincerely. He doesn't cover the bad with roses and pretty words because he has nothing to hide. He's a person who loves to give and respects my opinion; he values others besides himself. We both had a scratch on our hearts when we met. We burned with love, but we were frightened to trust each other. It took time to gain trust and erase the pain. It took time to erect a bridge connecting us. When we finally did, I was able to build my castles, walk on thorns, and create a loving home.

Everyone receives one or many lessons in life. We learn when we are young; we learn even when we think we know everything. One important lesson we need to learn is to respect and love ourselves. Each of us is unique and beautiful in his own way and deserves to be loved.

Girls, look in the mirror. See your beautiful eyes longing for flowers from the person you love. Look at your cheeks that someone likes to caress, and your lips thirsty for kissing. View your slender shoulders and your hands that caress, help the sick, build hospitals and theaters, draw the world, and groom loved ones. Each of us is a universe full of love, dreams, desires, sighs, and bitterness.

Life is to live and if we find someone who wants to share these dreams, pains, anger, and tortures with us without asking for anything but to love us for who we are, then we've found love. Love or affection, both are inherent in people. Let's find them.

Every Palm Sunday, I've tried to explain to my children what Flower Day is and why we celebrate. I try to preserve the traditions passed on from generation to generation. It's difficult for them to understand because they not only live and have been raised in another environment and culture, but also have had limited opportunities to be with their grandparents. I try to introduce them to the Bulgarian traditions, but also give them the opportunity to be part of the new culture in which they live and to respect all people's perceptions and differences.

Think about a single day here in America. We meet different people while shopping, at the spa, on the beach, at work, in the library, and many other places. At least a few of those people we meet will be of different origins, each of them having their own understanding, beliefs, customs, and rituals.

When we are open to diversity, we see people from different angles and accept them as equal to us. Whenever anyone asks me where I'm from, I tell them and then ask the same question back, because everyone has come from somewhere in the last twenty years, or fifty, or a hundred.

I light the wax candle which is on the ritual bread. I make a cross over the bread and sit at the table with my girls, my "flowers," and my companion in life, my beloved husband. My brother, his family, and my mom are not at the table with us, but they're in my heart.

We bring glasses of sparkling wine and toast each other Bulgarian style: "Cheers to all flowers, love and dignity!"

Chapter 6: Proshka – the Art of Forgiveness

The weak can never forgive.
Forgiveness is the attribute of the strong.
—Gandhi

Life is like a boat journey down an unknown river. With each phase of our life, we rise and fall along with the currents. Some parts of our travel may be obscured as we drift along, veiled in a mist, making decisions difficult. At times we may be stuck in a rut, unwilling or unable to get ahead; at other times, we're moving every minute of every day.

Life is dynamic.

At each step of this journey, something new happens to us. We discover things we love, other things that make us happy or miserable.

We meet new people. When we're born, we get to know our parents. As we grow up, we encounter kids at school, on the street, at college. We discover new people at work or social events. Some become our friends, others remain just people we know, and still others pass without a trace in our life.

Very often, loved ones, friends, or family hurt us. Some do it on purpose; others are stupid or just make a mistake. When you're abroad, far away from your home country, your parents, and relatives, the people around you and your friends become your family.

Since we arrived in America, we've made and lost several friendships. We've suffered a lot of disappointments from many people. But we've also found friends with whom we share celebrations, share our food at Easter, dance the horo, celebrate Christmas, and so much more. These are people who also have helped us in difficult moments. I think some of them have been in our life for more than twenty years. In hard times, woes, and joys. We raised our children together, built our lives together, and passed through the hardships of immigrant life. Perhaps because we are a handful of people, far from friends and relatives, we strive to support one another and live in harmony.

According to Orthodox tradition, every spring before Easter, we ask our relatives for forgiveness. We also call our parents and other relatives in Bulgaria and ask their forgiveness. Even if we haven't hurt or offended them, we use it as a way to get rid of the negative energy in our lives.

Forgiveness! What is forgiveness? Is it meaningless words? Is it enough to say or write words of apology in a text message or on social media? Or say the words over the phone?

When people hurt you, you feel angry; you're hating them for what they did to you. To forgive someone is not a simple act. It's not just saying the words "I forgive you." You need to change your heart toward someone—overcoming your feelings. You need to be strong to forgive. It's easy to say, but it takes time to feel it. Unforgiveness is like a heavy chain dragging after you, a scar from a scab you see every day, reminding you of the wrong someone did to you.

It's important to differentiate between forgiveness and trusting someone again. Can you forgive a person when he hurt you several times? If you do, does it mean you approve of his actions? Are you giving this person permission to hurt you again? Some people don't change for the better; they become more self-centered.

You can forgive, but you don't have to forget.

Forgiveness is an important part of our lives. It's no wonder Bulgarians, like other Orthodox, have a celebration called Proshka, Forgiveness. On the church calendar, this occurs before the Easter fast begins. The idea is to cleanse not only the body, but also the soul.

Although the church and other rituals were strictly forbidden during the Communist era in Bulgaria, my grandmothers honored them rigorously and taught us children to honor them. Before dinner, we had to kiss their hand and ask for forgiveness from them and our parents. It wasn't just words; it was a serious matter. I saw the respect and dignity on their faces as we paid our respect.

Afterwards, for my cousins and me, the day was like a party. My grandmother made her delicious round bread, cooked fresh eggs, baked banitsa, and had homemade feta cheese and white halva. When she didn't have white halva, she used Tahan halva, but they both melted in our mouths. We all waited for the dinner to end so we could make a *hamkane*.

My grandmother tied a red thread to the end of the dough roller, like a wooden rolling pin. To the other end of the thread, she attached a piece of halva, a piece of cheese, or a hard-boiled egg. We children stood in a circle on the floor or around the table with our hands behind us. We eagerly awaited our grandmother to shake the thread and make the halva dance. Like kids in America playing a donut game or apple dunking, each of us struggled to bite into the halva and get it to stay in our mouths. My brother and my cousins always won.

Another event that took place that evening was that the hunters from the village fired off their rifles in their yards. We had no fireworks, so this was how they proclaimed the beginning of the Easter fast.

Baba always kept the fast. I loved to eat cheese and banitsa, and so I always failed. When I was older, I stayed with my parents in Sofia. My mother didn't practice these traditions. Years later, I studied at various boarding schools where such folklore and church rituals were forbidden. Every year in the spring before Easter, I felt that something was missing from my life. I longed for the tradition that had brought our family together and was a lot of fun. It was a reminder to respect not only our grandparents and parents, but everyone who crossed our path. Unfortunately, I never practiced this ritual at my house and never shared it with my children.

The most important part of the Proshka ritual was the bonfire and the horo dance. Boys and bachelors from the village gathered boughs for the fire, called *sirnizi*, and stacked them around the stake for a bonfire. They lit the fires on Sunday evening. People believed that wherever the light from the flames touched, there would be no hail. In the past, they performed this rite on high mounds around the village, but in my grandmother's village, they made the fire in a meadow.

Once the fire burned to embers, brave boys jumped over it for health. Watching the light from the embers and listening to the slow music of the tupan (drum), I always wanted to try dancing on the fire. My grandmother clutched my hand and didn't let me near the flames. "Be still. You're not a fire-dancer. Your mother will kill me if you get burned."

Later in the evening, music and dancing took place at the village square. Everyone performed a fast-paced horo, bouncy and energetic, in order to grow lush and tall. Like most of the rituals in the villages, it was for fertility and a bountiful harvest. Even the grandmothers jumped with surprising vitality and energy during the horo.

After this holiday, people couldn't celebrate or dance the horo until Easter, and during this time people fasted and didn't marry. It was a symbol of a period of dying, with resurrection happening on Easter.

On this day, my grandpa and his brother Ivan forgave each other in their own way. They went through the words of forgiveness, hugging and shaking hands, and the peace lasted between them for about a month. After Easter, the truce ended, and they resumed fighting over a corn field that was next to my grandpa's house. Neither of them could find the line dividing the field between them. They quarreled over the land, even physically beating each other.

My grandfather's entire family lived in a neighborhood called Brusnicka. The problem between the two brothers was created by their ancestor Kotze. A rumor said that he found a pot of gold and gave it to one of his sons, but the other children hid it under the old walnut tree in his yard. Other people said he buried the golden coins under the hearth.

The story ignited our imaginations, and my cousins and I played treasure hunters. We made maps and searched for the golden treasure. In the evening, we watched to see if a blue flame would flare up under the old walnut tree. This was a sign treasure was buried there. The only light, however, came from our captured fireflies.

A few years ago when I visited Bulgaria, my uncle (my mother's brother) gave me an old golden coin. It's been passed down from generation to generation. Perhaps it's from the gold of the family's founder. For me, it's a relic and a connection with the past. I'll treasure it and pass it on to my grandchildren.

Whether it's true or not about the treasure he found, he managed to create a home for his children, a place to look after them. Around the original house, the sons and their sons built more houses, stables, gardens, and vineyards. They built their lives.

Everyone planted a tree. As a saying goes, every man must plant a tree, build a house, and raise a son. I want to change this saying a little: plant a tree, build a house, and leave a trace of yourself behind. It can be a child or a legacy, something important that's a part of yourself.

Great-great-grandpa Kotze had chosen a good place for his home and his family. It was in the Balkans where the old Turkish road led to the capital of Sofia. It was a lovely place with lush meadows, rivers, orchards, and vineyards, and close to two springs.

The water from the springs was sweet, especially when my grandmother poured it into a beautiful, colorful clay jug. I had a little clay vessel, too, and I helped her when she walked to get fresh water for drinking and cooking. I followed her and asked thousands of questions to which she always had an answer.

Their place was beautiful. It still is beautiful, but now it's deserted, and the fields are desolate. The brothers' houses are overgrown with ivy and buckwheat, and vines are wrapped around the wooden fence. The well isn't visible. You can't reach the house, not even with your eyes. It's hidden behind the bushes.

But who has the time to plow and plant fields and vines in these modern times? The children and grandsons of Grandfather Ivan, my grandpa's brother, have scattered around the world: some in New Zealand, others in Greece. My side of the family lives in America. My brother is in Bulgaria.

Life takes place in the city, where my parents lived and worked their entire lives. That's where there's work, jobs, money; the economy is good in the city, and so the villages become desolate. They are slowly dying. Many other villages have deserted houses and fields as well. People, the blood and life of the village, leave the place dry like the pear in the yard of my grandmother's old house.

Forgive me, grandparents.

Chapter 7: Colorful Eggs and Sweet Memories

The gentle caress of the weeping willow's bright green branches relaxes me and makes me feel secure. My dog chases after me, stopping to sniff everything while he waits for my attention. Unfortunately, today I'm too busy to play. I pick willow branches, plus gather other interesting leaves from the ground. Orthodox Easter is this Sunday, and I want to use traditional dyeing methods to create patterns on the eggs. Bulgarian women here want to re-create the colors of the eggs we've made in Bulgaria years ago: rich red, green, and blue.

Holding the greenery in my hands, I return to the house. Packages of different colors for the eggs are strewn across the table. In addition, I have a food-coloring kit to make sure my red eggs are as red as they can be this year. No matter what I've tried in the past, they always looked a washed-out pink. This year, all of the materials are from a Greek store called Sofia; the owner assured me that this is "the red of the reds."

The warmth in the kitchen and aroma of caramelized sugar and vanilla make me crave a cup of black coffee. Why not? I have time to get everything ready, so I shouldn't stress. I've ordered the lamb from the butcher in the Greek neighborhood, and I've bought the eggs and the finest, pure-white flour for the *kozunak*, the traditional ritual sweet bread that I make every year. The lady who sold me the red material for the eggs also sold me a packet of yeast that, per her words, does miracles and will make the kozunak rise easily.

I have the walnuts and the raisins ready. I've sifted the flour three times to add air. I drink a few cups of coffee and check my Facebook page as I wait for the dough to rise five times while it sits in the eighty-degree room. Unfortunately, something's always missing, and the bread is just not what I expect. It's hard and crumbly.

Not everyone can make a kozunak. When I was a child, my grandmother gathered with a few neighbors, and the women made buns all day. She kept the room warm; she didn't let us run back and forth from outside to inside. We had to stay one place or the other. It was like a holy place for one day. She said the kozunak was like a newborn baby and needed special warmth and care. I don't know what her secret was, but she made delicious kozunak. To this day, I remember the aroma and the taste of the toasted, lightly caramelized crust. When I broke it, it was loose and soft, cuddly like cotton. Having a piece of the kozunak and a cup of fresh organic milk with a thick cream was enough to keep us kids happy and running on the street the entire afternoon.

Easter holidays in Bulgaria start with Lazarov Day (Lazar's or Lazarus' Day) and Tsvetnica (Flower Day) and culminate on Easter. These are the best spring holidays when nature wakes and everything comes back to life. People open windows, clean their houses, and go to church every Sunday. When I was a student, we were forbidden to attend church. Back in the Communist era, we were told we had to forget religion and traditions so as not to undermine the authority of the Party. Even so, we hid and walked to attend the service secretly, so we weren't expelled from school. The world is small, as we like to say, and one year, I stood side by side with my French teacher in church. She looked away from me with candles in her hands and pretended she didn't see me. I did the same. We both knew we needed to keep the secret.

In Sofia, the measures were quite strict, but in small villages and towns people were able to celebrate and attend church more easily. In the years when I studied in Sandanski, a small town in southern Bulgaria, a friend invited me to the holiday in one of the neighboring villages so that I wouldn't be alone at the boarding school. The alley was pretty: white houses stained with colored rugs, and yards arranged with flowers and greenery. The church stood at the entrance to the village on a small hill with a view to the nearby Struma River. After the liturgy, young and old went out and, instead of the traditional "knocking" of their colored eggs (that is, tapping them end to end), they began to throw them over the church roof. Then they went outside the church yard, set food on picnic tables, and the fun began. The people of southern Bulgaria were warm and hospitable, and I always felt at home during my school years. It eased my nostalgia.

Bulgaria is a small country, but every region, village, and town has its own rituals and beliefs. It was interesting to observe traditions by visiting families and places that were new for me. I think we all need to be open to new experiences and appreciate the beliefs of others. Each ritual or custom has a reason behind why it's performed.

Some of these traditions are regarding eggs, one of the most common foods at Easter, for Bulgarians and other nations as well. From ancient times, the egg has been a symbol of birth, resurrection, and eternal life—life and death—with a belief that the world was born from the golden egg, that is, the sun. The parts of the egg represent the four elements. The shell is symbolic of earth: the membrane represents air, the liquid is water, and the yellow yoke is the sun and thereby fire.

The time to celebrate in secrecy eventually passed, and after the change of government in October 1989, democracy brought back freedom. Everyone then had the right to practice their religion. Easter and all other holidays are impeccable for Bulgarians not only today, but also in the past.

When I was a child, from time to time I stayed with my grandparents in a village in northern Bulgaria. Easter in my memories was about colors and flowers. I remember Lazar's Day and the lazarki, a group of cheerful girls who walked from door to door to sing for the prosperity and health of the occupants. The girls carried baskets and dressed in traditional costumes, wearing wreaths made from flowers. At the time, I badly wanted to join them, but I was too young. When they arrived at our house, Baba went to the cellar and brought eggs, honey, and walnuts as gifts for the girls.

On Tsvetnica, the next day, we went to church to pray. For us, it was a double holiday because my grandmother's name was Tsvetana (which means "flower"), so we also celebrated her name day. On Flower Day she made me a wreath from willow branches and flowers so I would be slender and playful like the tree. After church, people came over to celebrate her name day. The feast was not as it is now. Back then, the doors were open for all guests—those expected and unexpected alike. They came in happy, bringing gifts and wishing her good health. Baba gave them red wine and home-baked bread and other meals she had prepared for her special day. Since it was Lent, people fasted and kept other prohibitions.

My grandmother used natural dye to color the eggs: beets for the red, onion pills for the orange, and gold from the seeds of the dill. She also used these natural colors to dye wool and cotton. She told us we needed to color the eggs before sunset on Maundy Thursday (the Thursday before Easter). If we couldn't color them on that day, we had to dye them without telling anyone. The reason for this was that we had to make sure the devil didn't discover us dyeing eggs on Friday or Saturday. If he did, he'd destroy the healing and protective powers those special eggs held.

I still generally dye the eggs on Thursday and always make a red egg special for God. Traditionally, this is the first red egg. It has magical, healing power; on Easter morning, I rub the egg against my children's cheeks and make a cross on their foreheads for health. We keep this red egg set aside for a whole year. Sometimes our kitten forgets it's a holy egg and breaks it early. When the kitten doesn't break it, we don't throw last year's egg away. Instead, we bury it in the garden for fertility.

The culmination of the Easter festivities happens on Sunday. In Bulgaria, we went to church and on the way back visited the graves of our closest relatives to give them food, eggs, and wine. At home, we gathered around the table, ate lamb specially prepared for this day, and we knocked eggs. The last kid with an unbroken egg was the hero of the day. These traditions are preserved here, too.

The Bulgarian church has an evening service; part of the service is to walk around the church with a lit candle. It's a spectacular, energizing ritual. After the service, everyone takes the candle home, so it will bring them health and well-being. We save it so we can light it on other holidays and birthdays as well. If there is no Bulgarian church, Serbian, Russian, and Greek Orthodox churches always keep their doors open for new pilgrims. God is one; it's important to be in his temple and honor him. Whoever can't go to the evening service can attend one on Sunday. The Serbian church also holds a festive lunch after the service. It's another occasion for people to gather around the table and celebrate life and friendship. The conversations are in Bulgarian, English, or Serbian, but everyone understands each other. Food and wine unite people no matter what their nationality or language is.

The Easter table is special. After we've finished our Lenten fasting, we're allowed to consume meat. This is the only day I make lamb. It's not popular with my family. Since we don't have relatives here, we usually meet with friends and go to the community picnic or just celebrate at home. The salads are ready for us to begin the meal. We toast each other for health, and recite the traditional "Hristos Voskrese" ("Christ is risen") around the table. Afterwards, we swap eggs and fight with them, like a game, tapping the tip of our eggs against everyone else's egg. Whoever lasts the longest without his egg cracking is the winner. "Knocking" or fighting with eggs and eating green salad with radish and sliced eggs is an obligatory part of the holiday.

With social media, we're connected with friends and family, exchanging wishes and pictures, and showing off our kozunak and colored eggs. It's like an "Easter Gallery." We greet each other with "Hristos Voskrese" and "Voistine Voskrese" ("He is risen indeed").

If the April weather is still cold, we set the table inside, but when there's no snow on the ground, we hide Easter eggs, chocolate eggs, and other surprises in the yard. When my kids and their friends were little, they walked around the yard with baskets and collected them. If the Orthodox Easter falls on a different day than the Catholic one, we celebrate both, so the Easter bunny can come with presents.

On Easter, I also use incense to clear evil forces out of the house. My children always say the house smells like a church. I'm not sure if there really are any evil spirits, but I like to open the windows to chase them away anyway. The incense makes the house smell holy. I feel like my home has been purified, and the dark winter days are behind us.

All our Easter festivities are filled with light and love. Nature wakes up, and everyone is looking forward to the coming summer and long, sunny days. People are craving light, joy, and love.

Chapter 8: Name Days – the Season to Cheer

Names are an important part of human life. They're thought to determine people's destiny and how they'll be accepted in society. There's a belief in Bulgaria that every person comes into this world with purpose and with their name.

Every nation gives children names based on their beliefs. Among Bulgarians, the most popular tradition is to baptize each new generation with the name of an ancestor. Reviving or repeating the ancestral name is a way to praise the ancestor, telling him you rely on his help for luck and the well-being of your home. Even naming the child with a name that has the same first letter is a sign of respect.

The most accepted people to name after, in order, are the child's paternal grandfather, paternal grandmother, maternal grandfather, maternal grandmother, and then uncles and aunts. Usually, if the baby is a boy, he is named after the grandfather, and if the baby is a girl, she is named after the grandmother. However, in both modern Bulgaria and abroad, the custom of naming the child after an ancestor is not observed anymore.

Today, some people even name the child after the person who will look after the child. A lot of grandmothers fly from Bulgaria to other countries to take care of their grandchildren and help the young family. As we know, the price for child care is unaffordable, well beyond our imagination. Having grandparents take care of the children not only saves money, it also provides the opportunity for them to share Bulgarian culture with their grandkids.

Bulgarians also name children after the saints, whose holidays span the church calendar. Name days are a tradition from time immemorial. In the olden times, people didn't know the date of their birth. No one issued birth certificates, and no electronic databases existed. Naming a child after the day of the saint helped them remember when a person was born. It was a simple way of life.

For example, my uncle was born on October 26, Dimitrovden (Dimitrov's Day for Saint Demetrius). Everyone expected him to be named Dimitar by canonical church law since he was born on the saint's day, and so he was.

Another example is if a woman's labor is difficult or the mother dies giving birth, the child is traditionally named after the Virgin Mary (Maria).

I violated these traditions when my first child appeared in this world on Blagovets, March 25, a sacred church holiday. I suffered a full day of pain and prayers. After I woke up from my surgery and met my daughter, I decided to name her after my husband, the man who shares my pain and joy and my crazy dreams even today. According to beliefs, a child should not be named after the parents, because the spiritual connection between them diminishes, and the names create conflicts. I was young and in love. Our child was like the flower of our love, and the name came naturally.

Many name days and saint holy days occur in winter. In the past, after harvesting, people rested during the cold season, so they had more time for celebrations. Several holidays, and the festivities associated with them, occurred from early fall and continued through the winter months.

The numerous name days during this time, both in the past and now, help to fill the dark months with cheer and light. Doors are open for friends and relatives, and tables are traditionally covered with red wine, appetizers, and salads.

I always look forward to Atanasovden (Atanasov's Day for St. Athanasius), which is celebrated on January 18. According to folklore, the saint is the protector of winter frosts, snow, and domestic animals. People who celebrate this day are not only those named after the saint, but also blacksmiths, ironmongers, and cutters, because St. Athanasius is their patron.

On this day, women knead traditional pitka breads and dip them with honey. In some areas in Bulgaria in the past, young people went to the meadow, hung swings, and glided through the air on them.

Having endured a few months of cold and darkness, I'm ready for spring. After St. Athanasius, the longer days feed me with energy. It's still cold, but a saying goes, "Atanas came – the summer came," so I know warmer weather is on the way.

Unfortunately, this saying isn't valid for New England. Winter here starts earlier than January and sometimes piles of snow are heaped up everywhere until late April. That's why the season of picnics and gardening and wearing white shoes here begins after Memorial Day.

In the past, the day of the saint, all saints, was an occasion to celebrate life and share with friends and family. Families left their doors open, and no one had to send invitations; everyone was invited to the feast. Only during a recession or war did these traditions occur less often. People didn't have bread and wine, and the doors of their homes were closed either because of lack of attention or because of sadness when a relative or son was lost in a battle.

The gifts were different, simple and practical, not as they are today. When I was a child staying in my grandmother's village high up in the mountain, people gave presents of towels, homemade woven aprons, and white *kenar* embroidered shirts. Kenar is a handmade material, a mixture of cotton and silk, and the shirts were beautiful works by Bulgarian women. The aprons were like paintings, each one containing a coded message or a parable, which was told by the colors and shapes. All winter, women weaved the legends and tales into fabrics and carpets.

Every single name day is special, with unique traditions, but my favorite is Nikulden (St. Nikolas' Day), on December 6. Perhaps it's because of fond memories from my childhood. Nikulden is not simply a name day, but also a day on which fishermen and bankers celebrate. Since Bulgaria has a border with the sea, fishing has been and still is an important occupation for the country. You'll find many churches along the Black Sea coast named after St. Nikolas.

My grandfather's name was Nicholas, so we celebrated his name day. Baba, my mother's mother, made bread called a *paraklis*, which was different from the round pitka. She baked it in a special clay pot covered with coals. While she baked the bread and cooked the carp, which was the traditional meal for the day, she told us the legend of St. Nikolas. Every year, we the children listened to her with rapt attention, our mouths open like small fish.

St. Nikolas and the Sinking Ship

Besides being a patron saint and family protector, St. Nikolas was a miracle worker. One story tells about him travelling to the Holy Land to visit Christ's tomb. A mighty storm arose on the sea. This particular storm was quite fearsome. Lightning struck a sailor, killing him instantly.

Terrified people ran around, not knowing what to do. Another sailor shouted, "The storm damaged the ship! We have to stop the water from pouring in, or we'll all drown!"

St. Nikolas prayed, "Lord, save your people. Show them your mighty power."

When he finished speaking, a huge silver carp jumped into the hole, stopping the water from coming into the boat. To this day, that's why people say the carp is St. Nikolas' servant.

The saint also performed another miracle. He placed his hands on the dead sailor and again raised his voice to God. "Lord, return your servant to this world so he may continue to support his family."

The man immediately sat up. He looked around, stunned. The storm had quieted, and people were cleaning up the damage.

That's why we revere him as patron of sailors and fishermen. However, when he's angry, he can also send storms and hurricanes to punish people. The feast in his honor is performed to appease him. People pray to him to help and protect us, and also ask him to pray to the Lord for our forgiveness.

My mother was named after her father, so she also celebrated St. Nikolas Day. When I was with my parents during this time, the biggest attraction was to go out and choose the carp for our meal. We went to a fish shop in Sofia, opposite the former Communist Party central meeting house. I stood in front of the big windows, with my nose glued to the glass, so I could see the fish swimming. In the way of a child, I imagined the fish were talking to me as they opened and closed their mouths.

After my father chose our carp, on the way back we stopped at a shop where he usually bought me a chocolate bar as a reward. It was winter, and in the nearby specialty shop exotic fruits covered the entire showcase window. I looked at the oranges and the bananas, my mouth watering. I swallowed, but I didn't say a word. I was pleased to have chocolate that I could share with my brother. I squeezed the bar in my hand and walked along with my father.

Later, my mother cooked the carp, filling it with rice, raisins, walnuts, and a mix of spices. She also made salads and set the table with pickles and sour cabbage. The carp went well with rakia, the spicy Bulgarian brandy. The table was filled with chatter, songs, and cheers. Music played on a gramophone, or my talented dad played the accordion. We all sang urban songs that kept the mood of our company cheery, letting them forget their pain and misery.

The tradition stopped when I lost my father. He suddenly passed away on his name day, so today, name days always remind me of this loss. I did preserve the tradition again in New England because it's a reason to relax, enjoy time with friends and family, and celebrate life, but I can't relinquish the bitterness in my soul.

Many of my new friends who aren't Bulgarian are amazed at name day celebrations when I share our traditions and the reason we're celebrating. We invite friends to the house; we cook, eat, and drink.

Since St. Nikolas is the protector of fishermen, men tell their own fish tales, competing about who caught the biggest fish. We all listen to their colorful stories and pretend we believe them all.

We all look forward to the traditional stuffed carp. Everyone takes a fish bone to put on a bracelet for luck and wealth. In olden times, women took the bone that looks like a cross and sewed it into a newborn's cap so St. Nikolas would protect the infant and keep him healthy.

The next day I carefully fold my fishbone into a napkin and put it into my purse for money and luck. On my way to work, I go to the nearest gas station to buy a lottery ticket and try my luck. Who knows? I may have the winning ticket.

Chapter 9: White Roses

"If you ever feel distressed during your day—call upon our Lady—just say this simple prayer: 'Mary, Mother of Jesus, please be a mother to me now.' I must admit—this prayer has never failed me."
—Blessed Mother Teresa

Great men and women are the force behind progress; they lead revolutions or social reforms, discover new lands, and travel into space. Some plan to colonize planets, others to build schools in Africa or save polar bears in the arctic North Pole regions. Many other people like us quietly live their lives, raising children and working at the same job for more than forty years with pride in our quality work. These people are not visible to the world, but they're part of the success of our society. And who demonstrates this better than mothers?

We love mothers. Mother's Day is the single busiest day for phone calls home to that special lady. Mom is our temple, the first person we met when we arrived in this world. Her love is unconditional all our lives, and she's ready to give her life for her child.

While I was working on this chapter, another shooting, actually two mass shootings, happened one after another. One in El Paso, Texas, and one in Dayton, Ohio. Why would I even mention these horrible events? While I was watching the news, they were talking about a little two-month-old baby whose mother shielded him, and the gunmen took her life. This is what a mother does: she protects, she loves, and she is ready to die to save her child.

If you ask my children about me, I'm sure they'll say I'm demanding, powerful, and sometimes mean, or that I expect the impossible from them. When they were growing up, it was hard for me to say "good job" on a school grade just because other moms were saying this to their kids. For me to give them this praise meant what they did had to be excellent, an A or above. I know I've been tough, and sometimes expected too much from my daughters. I even have called myself "the dragon mother."

I think this is typical for Bulgarian mothers living abroad who were born and raised in Bulgaria. We want to make sure our kids get accepted to quality schools and the most acclaimed ivy-league colleges. We help them do what they need to so they can win scholarships, get the best education, choose a great career that they'll love, learn foreign languages, and overall be successful in life. We push them hard to work and study as we do, to make sure they're winners. I don't know if this is wrong or right. I guess it's likely to be cultural.

Even if we planned everything and hoped for success, life is an unpredictable journey. It throws everyone ups and downs: we win, we lose. But mothers are like a safe harbor, a sanctuary we can seek to get support, forgiveness, and courage. When life has been difficult, or if I've needed advice, I've reached out to my mother many times. She never asks or judges; she just supports me.

A famous Bulgarian song, "Prituri se planinata," is about two shepherds trapped in a mountain with a storm coming. They ask the mountain to help them. They want to go back to the people waiting for them. One of them desires to return to his mother, the other to his wife, his first and only love. The mountain responds by telling them she will let go only one of them, the one whose mother is waiting for him. A mother, she says, waits and mourns all her life, but a wife will be sad for a while and then find another love. It's a powerful song, showing again the love of the mother and how it's portrayed in Bulgarian folklore.

Притури се планината
Притури се планината,
Че затрупа два овчеря.
Че затрупа два овчеря,
Два овчеря – два другаря.

Първи моли, пусни мене.
Мене чака първо любе.
Втори моли, пусни мене.
Мене чака стара майка.

Проговаря планината:
Хей, ви вази два овчеря,
Любе жали ден до пладне,
Майка жали чак до гроба.

The mountain has overturned (collapsed)
The mountain has overturned
And captured two shepherds.
And captured two shepherds.
Two shepherds, two friends.

The first one begs: "Let me go!
My first love is waiting for me!"
The second one begs: "Let me go!
My old mother is waiting for me!"

The mountain replies:
"Oh, you two shepherds,
A beloved one grieves from morning till noon
but a mother grieves for life!"

Mothers are strong, the cement holding families together. Many novels and stories demonstrate the power of women, especially mothers, in world literature: *A Tree Grows in Brooklyn*, the *Little House on the Prairie* series, and *Little Women*, to name a few. From Bulgarian literature, I can add my favorite tale, "Mother's Tear."

Being a woman and a mother is even harder when you're an immigrant. You need to work, take care of the family, and overcome obstacles presented by the new culture. One of the roles of a mother is to introduce her children to family traditions, their roots, but also help them embrace their new culture. It's hard to do in this high-tech world where lifestyles and communication tools are different from those in your home country.

In the past, we read newspapers and print books, and we went to libraries. Today our kids use smart phones and ask Siri questions, or type in information on Google to find what they need. Many have never even talked to a librarian or sorted through a card catalog the way we used to when we were working on school research papers.

Even though the social dynamics are different today, we need to preserve our culture, our family rituals, making sure our children know their heritage. Knowing who you are and where you come from helps you build your future and gives you identity. This is why I started writing stories and books inspired by Bulgarian folklore and customs. I wanted my children and other people to learn more about Bulgaria, so they can respect my culture. I think we all need to respect and learn about the people around us, the new people we meet every day. Don't judge people by their appearance, accent, or color. Take the time to learn about them. Each person has a story, dreams, and ambitions.

In my family, I honor and practice the major Bulgarian holidays, but we also celebrate American holidays and adopt new rituals. When we came here in 1998, it was fall. I hardly spoke or understood English, but I was able to discover that a holiday called Halloween was approaching, and that I needed to buy candy and dress up the kids. We got costumes and candies. I put on makeup and turned myself into the Wicked Witch of Oz. Even my husband wasn't able to recognize me; I scared the hell out of him. The lady next door handed us candy and was able to recognize me after I spoke to her, because of my accent. It was a fun experience.

We still celebrate Halloween. Every year I wait with a bowl of candy and candy bars to see the excited little pumpkins, dressed like butterflies, cats, dragons, monsters, and more. Lately, people want to cancel these celebrations at schools because some parents are offended. I don't think it's offensive. I think it's just another reason to open your home to people, meet the kids on your street, and be social. I think we need to respect the current traditions and holidays and continue to observe the ones from our heritage as well.

The same controversy surrounds the Christmas tree. Some people aren't happy that it's called Christmas, so they want to call it Holiday! Holiday? Please leave the Christmas tree alone. It's a special tree we light up every year to celebrate the birth of God and the beginning of a new cycle of life. In America, everyone is supposed to be able to celebrate their religion and observe their holidays. Keep your beliefs, traditions, and religion, but also respect the current customs.

In Bulgaria and in Europe, Mother's Day is on March 8. This is the day when everyone appreciates their mothers and says thank you for their hard work. I still celebrate on March 8 and also on the American Mother's Day in May. Celebrating in May helped my children feel the same as their classmates. They make me lovely cards, and we go out for lunch.

On Mother's Day, I get a bouquet of white roses, my favorite flowers, from my husband. A white rose is the flower of the Virgin Mary, the mother of God, our Mystical Rose of Heaven. For me, Mother's Day isn't about being one day in the year when you get cards, kisses, and flowers.

Every day when you know you've raised good children is Mother's Day. Every day we celebrate the love, the pain, the sleepless nights, the cheers.

    We grow, we make friends; we move, we lose many of them. As time passes, it's more and more difficult to make new friendships. But also with time, we become wiser and gain the ability to appreciate and respect the people around us. We begin to understand that our mother has always been and will always be our best friend in life.

    Our mothers are our white roses.

Chapter 10: Fearless

My throat was covered with dust. I could barely breathe in the dark cavern of the truck. Carton after carton was passed to my hands. The wall of cardboard boxes that I was stacking grew bigger and bigger. Some were light, while others slipped from my hands and hit the wooden floor with a crash, scattering sawdust and bits of paper. I tried to stop to rest, but the stream of packages and cartons sputtered down the line like the throat of a large iron dragon. Outside the truck, in the vast building, endless conveyors intertwined like tentacles and formed a metal tangle. If any workers stopped, the cartons still squirmed, falling onto the floor to overwhelm them.

Suddenly, the line stopped as it did from time to time when the boxes jammed. It was an opportunity to take a short break, sit down on the floor to relieve your back. Unfortunately, it was a few minutes before four in the morning, and my shift was almost done. I didn't have time for a break. I had a pile of boxes waiting on the floor around me.

A tall figure of a man came in and approached our group. His face was in the shadows, but I thought I'd seen him before. "Good morning! Why are we late, and why are so many boxes and packages on the floor?"

He twisted a small package still on the conveyor. He approached me and kicked the wall of boxes I had stacked for hours. It collapsed. Boxes with Dell's emblem scattered around him. "Didn't they teach you how to make a proper wall?"

His angry voice made me ill. It took a huge effort to lift all those packages to build that wall, and now they were rolling on the floor.

With my broken English, I tried to explain to him. "They have studied us, but these boxes are of different size and difficult to arrange. At the same time the flow is unrepresented. I have no time." He didn't understand that I was telling him I was trained how to stack the boxes, but the different sizes and the unending flow of boxes made it difficult to keep up.

"Don't explain to me. Start over. The truck leaves in two hours. If you fail to load it on time, it's over. Don't come to work tomorrow."

"But my shift is up at 5 a.m. I have to—"

"I don't want to hear it. Keep loading the truck and don't be late."

I wiped sweat from my forehead, switched on the scanner again, and shook as I rearranged the wall of boxes. Drops of sweat ran down my back. I paused long enough to gulp from my bottle of Gatorade until it was empty.

Luckily, the shipment on this line was small that night. It was the slow season, and I was able to load the truck before 5 a.m. When I finished, I ran toward the building's exit, punched my card, and removed the scanner from my wrist. My car was at the far end of the parking lot, and it took a while to get there. Finally, I was inside the vehicle and heard the roar of the engine as I turned the key. It was an old car, but still reliable.

I drove home quickly. Warmth flooded the car as the heater kicked in. It was comforting, but my head drooped and my eyes closed from fatigue a few times. Panicking, I opened the window. The icy breeze refreshed me for a moment, but again I felt fatigue knocking me out. I knew it was dangerous to drive in that condition, but I didn't have time to stop and rest. It was getting late, and I needed to get home.

When I parked the car in front of the apartment building, all the windows were dark. I quietly unlocked the building's front door and climbed to our third-floor apartment. I unlocked our door, and warmth splashed across my face, bringing with it the savory smell of toasted bread. A plate with food was waiting for me on the table. My husband hugged me with a cup of coffee in his hand. I wasn't hungry, but the black aroma of the coffee smelled good.

The children were still asleep. I washed and changed my clothes and started to make breakfast before I woke them. They had thirty minutes to eat and get ready for school and kindergarten.

Their laughter and smiling faces made me forget the pain in my back, my wounded pride, the burning in my red eyes, and my hands scratched from lifting so many parcels.

We didn't have much money, but toys made my young children carefree and smile. I wanted them to be happy, so the first thing we bought them was a big kitchen set and a doll house. The doll house was beautiful, with three floors, furniture, and lights. Sometimes I wanted to live there, remembering our home in Bulgaria. Most of the time, work kept me too busy to be sad, and I was able to kill my feeling of nostalgia. I also occupied my mind by learning.

This morning was the same as every other one for the last several months. My husband worked long hours during the day, so we saw each other just to say hello and goodbye and surrender our children to each other. We met in the kitchen, embraced, and wished one another a nice day with a kiss. The children like kittens ran giggling down the stairs after him.

After he left for work, I ran with them to the bus stop, holding their lunch boxes in one hand and my cup of coffee in the other. I sat at an angle on the bench, listening to the other mothers enjoying their conversations.

They glanced at me, but never talked to me. I was a stranger who couldn't speak their language well. It was easier for me just to smile and wave.

As soon as my munchkins were on the bus, I ran as fast as I could back to the apartment. I grabbed my pile of textbooks and got into the car. I had to hurry. My first class at a nearby community college was in thirty minutes, and I had a test.

Test ... I had a test! I was stressed, but I had no time to think about it. I started the car and headed for the college. My head felt heavy with fatigue, and thoughts scrambled my brain.

Fortunately, the test was easy and to my surprise I got a good grade. The next classes after that one were a nightmare: my head kept nodding and my eyelids closed with fatigue. I watched the clock, waited for noon. Finally, the last class was almost over. It took a lot of effort to hold in my yawn.

I hurried back to the bus stop and made it in time for the bus. I waved to my kids and held them as they scrambled off. Back at home, they promised to play quietly. But I was so tired, it was hard for me to sleep. I knew I needed to, because my body was exhausted, but my brain still thought about a million things: school, my mother's sad face when we left, my boss kicking the boxes in the dirty truck.

The day was over by the time my husband returned. It was time for me to once again climb into the dark, dirty truck and build wall after wall of boxes until the first roosters crowed.

That all happened twenty years ago when we had to learn to survive in this new country. To get a loan or rent an apartment, my husband and I had to have a credit history and full-time jobs. Being new to the country, we didn't have either. At that time, there weren't many Bulgarians in the area, and it was hard to find a guarantor. Fortunately, the owner of a local company was a Bulgarian and knew my husband's name from the sports newspapers. He helped him get a job in his factory, and we were able to secure the apartment.

When we first came here, I found a job in a restaurant. I needed something. It was a low-paid position, but it was a job. I used to work for an international bank and travel a lot. My last job in Bulgaria was an auditor, a stressful job during a political period of change in the country. When I took the waitress job in America, I thought it would be easy in comparison. I was surprised to find how challenging it was with the culture and language differences. One thing I've learned all these years is that for each job you need a skill and you need to like what you're doing.

I still tell a funny story to my kids and friends about the time when I was a waitress. A customer ordered a ginger ale, but I thought she said "a jingle bell" and wondered if she were asking for a song. I rushed to the kitchen and using hands and some English was able to explain that the customer was asking for a Christmas song. Everyone looked puzzled. Luckily, the friendly chef was helpful, and he explained that they probably asked for a drink called ginger ale. He went and gave the group a special appetizer and talked to them to make sure his assumption was right. He was right; the person had asked for soda. Twenty years later, the story makes me laugh. Back then, I was frustrated and ready to quit, but I didn't.

Things are different now. Many Bulgarians who arrive with green cards are starting a good job their first week, and their lodgings aren't a problem. Large Bulgarian communities in residential complexes recommend each other. The place where we lived eventually turned into a small Bulgarian community with at least ten more families—each brought there by the recommendation of someone else.

At the beginning, my job at UPS was hard, but it was a good opportunity. I was a student during the day, and they paid for my classes. At night, I loaded trucks to make money and help with the bills.

My shiny diploma from Bulgaria didn't impress anyone here. I was an economist, but I discovered programmers could find work easily, even without a graduate diploma. For that reason, I went back to school and started learning a new profession.

After I completed a college certificate program, I was able to find a good job. My luck ran out when the Internet bubble collapsed, and I lost my job. The bills kept coming in, so I had to find a few gigs working as a contractor. I promised myself I'd keep moving and complete a second degree. It took a lot of deprivation: lack of sleep and valuable time that I could have spent with my children.

On some evenings, the Boston rats were the only living creatures to keep me company on the empty city streets. After a long day of work, I could relax as I sat in the empty compartment on the last train from North Station. I leaned my head against the window. My breath formed ice-cold snowflakes on the glass. My stop was the next to last, and my car was the last one left in the deserted parking lot. With frozen hands, I unlocked the door and drove home.

Moments later, my girls' hugs returned me to my world, where it was warm and beautiful, full of loving and caring. Too often, all I could do was put my head on the pillow with the last of my strength. I felt guilty for being too tired to read them fairy tales. I hope that by the time I become a grandparent, I'll have the opportunity to do this for my grandchildren.

Despite the obstacles, I managed to earn two degrees and graduate from elite colleges. At the last ceremony, I walked with the other students from my class and was glad to see the faces of my girls in the audience. I was sure they were proud of me, and they would follow my example.

Life can be an obstacle to achieving objectives, but when one has a goal, he can obtain it. Neither heavy UPS boxes nor nightmares, ignorance of language and local culture, or other difficulties have scared or deterred me. I had goals. I had to survive to achieve each one of them. I had to concentrate so I could continue to establish myself as a professional person, build my career, and take care of my family. Years later, when I attended the graduation ceremony for my children, I saw the fruit of my efforts.

It's hard when you're in a new environment, and you don't know how to reach out to people and ask questions to find simple things. You don't know what is allowed and what can be misinterpreted by your colleagues and friends. When you say a word, it sounds strange and unrecognizable to everyone. Or you say your name a few times before people can pronounce it or write it in their meeting notes. When they get tired of asking how to say my last name, they use only my first name.

Maybe that's why I've always been attracted to diverse teams and diverse cultures. Everyone in the team has a different background. They try harder to understand what you mean, and your accent doesn't feel so harsh and noticeable during collective talks because everyone has their unique accents. When you have an accent, people are forced to listen to you more carefully so they'll understand.

After twenty years of studying, working, learning, and listening, I'm still nervous when I write emails or do a simple presentation. I measure each word several times, but when I have to answer several emails quickly, I make mistakes that hurt my professional image. I tend to underestimate myself, believing I'm not qualified to do the task.

When I ask for a promotion or apply for a new job, I remind myself of where I'm coming from: the flying parcels, the hungry rats in the deserted Boston streets, and the cold wind piercing my bones. It motivates me to expect people to respect my achievements. I appreciate what I've accomplished with deprivation, labor, and patience.

Fearless. That's a word I heard from a female friend from Taiwan. It's stuck in my mind. She, too, has gone through the thorny path of success. She's now a successful dentist, but twenty-five years ago when she arrived here, she wasn't. She has built her practice at the center of a prestigious city. She's a professor at one of the best colleges in Boston. She also likes to say, "Never give up; always have an outlet."

She and I have different destinies, but we are both fearless women, two of many others who exist.

Fearless.

Chapter 11: Horo – the Circle of Love

The modern Bulgarian horo is as diverse as we ourselves are, a rainbow of colors and music. It's more than a circle dance; for me, it's a circle of love and unity. We dance the horo at weddings, name days, and even funerals as we say our last goodbye to friends and loved ones while sending them into eternity. The circle and holding hands represent the unity of the community.

In the past, people assembled at the village square to celebrate important holidays like St. George's Day, on May 6, and Easter. Under Communist rule, however, the only major holiday people were allowed to celebrate officially was September 9, the day of the Party's victory.

The horo was a central part of these events. Besides dancing, it was a social gathering, a place for young people to meet and talk, and get to know each other as part of the engagement process. These traditions may still be preserved in small villages throughout Bulgaria.

When I was a child, in the village where my grandmother lived, the locals performed live music at the central plaza called Megdan. Everybody celebrated and danced, chatted and laughed. Each person felt the equal of all the others when people danced the horo. Poor and wealthy, Communist and kulak (well-off peasant), everyone was the same. In a circle, holding hands, smiling, looking into each other's eyes, they forgot their enmity.

My grandmother's inn was at the center of the village, so the music, the horo, and all other festivities were always happening at her front door. Even though she wasn't happy with the current Communist regime, she loved to dance and laugh and be with other people. As the horo wound its way in front of her house, she joined in the dance and held hands with friends and enemies. She smiled and raised her head, her laughter echoing over the Klisura section of the village of Lutti Dol.

Baba encouraged me to dance and I tried, tapping and jumping with my new shoes and spinning in my favorite dress. Unfortunately, to this day, I can dance only the basic straight "pravo" horo, which has simple steps. Even though I'm not a skilled dancer, I always join the circle of unity and joy when people dance at events. No one will judge you or assess your skill during the horo. People around you accept and encourage you to learn. I watch the feet of the person next to me, following their steps. Even without doing that, I find the music and high energy level make it easy to follow along and learn.

For people who aren't accustomed to Bulgarian culture, their first impression of the dance is that we merely jump and scream. There's more to it than that; meaning and rhythm hide within each dance.

My knowledge and reflection on this subject come from conversations I've had with people in villages, my own experience, and from people who have dedicated their lives to preserving these mystical rituals and traditions, which they've carried abroad.

I call the dance a ritual because it's a sacred tradition we inherited from the Thracians, who inhabited Bulgaria and other lands thousands of years ago. The horo was a way for them to connect the material world to their spiritual life, which is encoded in the dance's rhythms. For the Thracians, among whom is Orpheus, the famous musician born in the Rhodopes, the music was what connected mankind with their spiritual reality.

The music of the horo has a specific rhythm. The most popular is 7/8, which we Bulgarians know as our *ruchenitza* or a rhythmic dance in pairs. Within this rhythm is the vibrating of the cosmic spheres, like the sun, which held a sacred role in Thracian beliefs and rituals. Like the sun sends out two short, then one long pulse, so does the human heart work.

I once came across an exhibition dedicated to the horo that was on display on the streets of Veliko Tarnovo, the old capital of Bulgaria. The paintings presented in the exhibition were made from the footprints of the rhythmic horo dancers. I was shocked by the symbolism encoded in every dance.

Some of the footprints resembled the fiery summer sun shining on our ancestors in the fields: the sun with its burning rays, the sun that gives light and brings everything to life. Others reminded me of the embroidery in the Bulgarian *shevitza* geometric designs, which have been preserved for centuries. Some designs were in the shape of a snowflake. Another one reminded me of the Eniovden (Midsummer's Day) wreath, in which women weave together seventy-seven and a half herbs gathered during the first magical rays of the sun on June 24.

In the past, a strict structure about the performance of the horo was passed from generation to generation. Based on the old canons, young, unmarried women perform the first one. Following them, bachelors dance. Next come married women, whose horo is more relaxed, slow, and dignified. Finally, all the men perform after having a feast at the local tavern. They embark on their "heavy" *chorbadji* horo; the steps are slow, with the men holding hands or shoulders, and the music is melancholy.

The structure of the horo represents the hierarchy of the Bulgarian family. The person who leads the dance usually is the oldest or most honorable man in the community, or it's led by the most authoritative man in the village, often the mayor himself. Next come the married men who are ranked by age. After them are the bachelors. The women's lineup mirrors that of the men: first those who are married, then the single women. Finally, at the end are the children. The last in the line, according to tradition, will be a boy.

Even abroad today, the horo is a gathering of both acquaintances and strangers. My non-Bulgarian friends accept it with interest and wonder when I explain that there really are no rules today. I tell them they can join this circle of positive energy without permission even if they don't know anyone at the event. They don't have to worry that they may be unwanted because everyone is welcomed to join the circle at any point during the dance and leave when they want to. The important thing is to preserve the integrity and unity of the circle.

There is no division between those who are capable and those who dance poorly, those who are experts or mere beginners. Anyone who can't dance is given the opportunity to learn. If he is blind, he can hear the music and dance. If he doesn't speak the language, he will learn the steps because music doesn't have to be translated.

The dance is energizing. Sometimes, even if I'm out of breath, I'll continue to dance. I don't feel fatigued, though; quite the opposite, I'm refreshed and energized. Perhaps this is because the horo is said to cure people and chase away evil.

Even though we don't have many opportunities to practice the horo, I did have a chance to teach Bulgarian dances to kids in Guard Up!, a Boston-based organization. They arrange summer camps for children to learn about other cultures. I worked with them on a volunteer basis and introduced the children to Bulgarian rituals and mythology, including the story about the powerful and evil female dragon called *lamia*. One of the evenings was dedicated to Bulgarian folk music and dance and its magical impact.

To my surprise, the program director asked me to introduce the *kalushari* dance to the children. After several conversations with Bulgarian choreographers in Boston, I learned they had no knowledge about the dance. I decided to do online research, watch YouTube videos, and present my discoveries to the children.

Nowadays, the ritual is performed at festivals. Usually a group of three, five, or most often seven people perform the dance. According to folklore, only men, called kalushari (those who know the secrets of magical healing), participate. I was afraid I was breaking the canon by being a woman taking part in the dance.

The men wear ordinary, white embroidered shirts and have healing herbs on their caps and bells on their boots. They carry wooden sticks, with a sharp iron spike at the bottom, which they dig into the ground during the ritual dance. I used a stick, but, to make the presentation more exciting, I decided the kids could use plastic swords since they had them as part of another game.

In the past, the dance was performed not only for health and fertility, but also for the treatment of sick people. The melody of the dance was a particularly strange form of *ruchenitza* but more frequent, which one person playing the bagpipe performed. Ruchenitza is the fastest and can be perform by two people, female and male, dancing facing each other, or as a horo circle dance. People think that the ruchenitza is the fastest horo, but there are two types of ruchenitza: Thracian ruchenitza and Shoppe ruchenitza. The Thracian dance is slow and the steps are low, while the Shoppe is faster. People dance with higher steps and quick, bouncy rhythms. The role of the melody in this ritual was to make the kalushari fall into a trance, during which time they connected with the supernatural powers of nature.

After weeks of work and training at home under my husband's and girls' stunned looks, I was able to perfect the magical steps of the dance. I had made my own version, but kept its authenticity as much as possible. I managed to find mystical music to complement the dance. In the process of preparing for the program, I decided to also teach the kids one more type of horo for the end of the event, the standard horo.

I wondered how the children, who had never heard of a horo and Bulgarian folk music, would accept the dance. To my surprise, they learned the dance on the fly, paying close attention as they watched every step I took. At the end of the night, they all were able to perform both dances.

My eyes teared up when I watched more than 200 children between the ages of ten and fifteen holding hands, dancing in a circle to the rhythm of Bulgarian folk music. When the music ended, everyone decided they wanted to repeat the dance. I received a lot of thanks after the event. I felt I was part of an important ritual, which I saw in the eyes of the children. I wish my own children would learn the dance and pass it on to their children, but time will tell.

Clubs and groups abroad teach people different folk dances, and talented, professional groups perform folk dances at festivals and events. One well-established ensemble, Ludo Mlado, was my guest at the presentation of my first book, *Mystical Emona: Soul's Journey*, at Boston

University. They enchanted the guests with a wonderful choreography of the Trakiski wedding and the mysticism of the Samodivi dance.

For years, in Chicago, the Vereya Festival is a prestigious place where groups and ensembles compete for an entire week every year. They bring their colorful costumes, music, and choreography to the public. It's a week filled with food for the soul and pleasures for the eyes.

No Bulgarian concert or picnic is conducted without a horo here. It's performed at the Rose Festival, St. George's Picnic on May 6, New Year's Eve, on Bulgarian Independence Day on March 3, and, of course, at private gatherings, graduation parties, and weddings.

The music makes old and young, Bulgarians and people from other heritages, join hands and dance until dawn.

Dancing the horo is a spiritual journey. It's interesting to note that the movement of the dance is from left to right or counterclockwise. *Nestinari* fire dancers also perform counterclockwise, and even the twirl of the banitsa pastry is counterclockwise. Perhaps the connection originates from the ancient Thracians. To them left was the spiritual, celestial, immortal direction, while right was earthly and mortal.

For me, the horo is a sacred rite of unity where energy throbs from the human palms, eyes, and smiles with immeasurable and refreshing power.

The circle of Love.

Chapter 12: Samodiva Cheshma – the Magic of Water

"Wind blows our footsteps—first the passions, then time swallows us. This fountain is built because the stone is more durable than we are, and the water is eternal."
—Unknown (carved on a cheshma)

Fountains (*cheshmas*) have a special place in the life and lifestyle of the Bulgarians. They not only bear life-giving water, but they can also be beautiful structures, legacies of what their builders have left behind. Planting trees, capturing water, and building fountains are well-known traditions in Bulgaria even today.

As a child, I had the opportunity to study in Tryavna, a beautiful town known for its wood-carving school, pretty houses from the Revival period, and clock tower. I stood at the bottom of the clock tower, looking at it with fascination for hours. Tryavna was the place where I first fell in love with wood and the magic of trees. I was about twelve years old, an age when we are still children but start to transform into adults. Watching the talented hands of the old masters at work made me decide to do woodcarving: tales made from a piece of walnut tree, history carved into wooden planks, all inspired me. When I first touched the chiseled wood, I felt its soul. Each piece of wood has a story to tell; you just need to discover it and show the world. My life changed after that. My chisels are now stored away in a box, but I'm sure one day I'll take them out when the time is right.

The soul of the past lives in other places in the town of Tryavna as well. During my stay, I learned a wonderful love legend. I often passed a white, marble fountain with a sculpted face of a beautiful maiden and a marble bench beside her. One day my art teacher told our class the legend of the secret love between a young woodcarver and the most beautiful girl from Tryavna. The young carpenter wasn't recognized as a master yet, so he lacked the courage to ask for her hand in marriage. Then he decided to show the local masters how talented he was and selected marble, the hardest material to work with. He created a fountain by sculpting the image of his beloved, and the water was a symbol of their eternally fused souls.

After the fountain was finished, he was accepted by the masters. He received not only their blessings, but also the girl's hand.

To this day, the water from this fountain flows throughout the year, and has never dried up. The legend tells that if someone takes a sip of that water, he drinks a piece of the love that remains forever within it. In Bulgarian folklore and literature, there are many songs and poems about fountains, or as we called them cheshmas. It's not difficult to understand because for the Bulgarian water is sacred, magical. Water has healing power.

The Sokolovski Monastery is located near the village of Tryavna. Why do I mention it?

There are many fountains throughout Bulgaria, but one that I admire the most is the one in the Sokolovski Monastery. It's in the middle of the monastery, built from a white stone fountain and has eight spouts.

During the April Uprising in 1876, rebels led by Tsanko Dyustabanov hid in a shelter in the Sokolovski Monastery. They were discovered, and eight of the rebels were captured, hanged, and their bodies thrown into a deep abyss in the monastery. As a symbol of this tragedy, the famous Bulgarian master builder Kolyo Ficheto built the stone fountain with eight falcons representing the heroes. The legend says the fountain never dries up, and its water has miraculous abilities to heal the sick and keep away evil spirits.

In legends and folklore, every water body has its own spirit. People believe that water sources, springs, rivers, and lakes are guarded by these beings. One of the most well-known of these spirits are the *rusalki*, often called mermaids. In their purest and oldest form, these water maidens represent fertility. They appear on land only one week out of the year in order to spread fertility over the land.

Terrifying songs and legends about fountains also exist, telling about how a girl's or woman's shadow (or even the person herself) has been built into the structure. According to folklore, when the construction of a bridge, house, or fountain occurs, the shadow of a person must be built into its foundation to make it strong. This is done by measuring the person or the shadow with a string and putting it into a box, which the builder encloses in the foundation. Usually this was a person passing by, in some legends a maiden or a mother with a child. After forty days, the person dies. Whether it's because of the ritual or not, these bridges and fountains have survived to this day and keep the legends alive.

Fountains and wells were also a meeting place for young people, or as we say today, a place they could go on a date. In Bulgarian folklore, wells were where the dragon *zmey* waits for his beloved maiden to come so he can make her his wife.

Other legends talk about a water *stopan* (guardian spirit) or water buffalo that guards treasures. When I was little, my grandmother sent me for spring water in a place called Bivola (Buffalo). The fountain had three spouts, which were stopped with wooden plugs to keep the water from running all the time. An old willow grew beside the fountain. No one knew how old it was, but it could have been more than five centuries old.

The water was clear as a tear, sweet and cold. We used a pottery vessel called *stomna* to carry the water. It kept it fresh for a few hours. Baba told us not to go to the fountain in the dark, saying that Bivola would come out and take us away to protect the hidden treasure. We children drew maps and made up stories, but we never tried to dig around the willow to discover the treasure.

The term "silent water" occurs frequently in folk tales. What this means is that people must carry water back from a spring in complete silence. It's believed that on some holidays this water and dew have healing power. In the past, people in villages used such water when they made ritual bread. Silent water is also used to keep away *uroki*, evil spirits or "the evil eye," or any bad person who looks at you and gives you bad energy. Usually, people affected by a uroki suffer from headaches and fever, and their faces become red.

When our heads hurt, our grandmother would remove the uroki and fever by taking an ember from the hearth and murmuring something with a low voice. I caught the words zmey (dragon) and eagle. She made a cross three times and dropped the ember into the water. If the sizzle was strong, it meant we had been *urochasan* (that is, have been spelled by the "evil eye"). She had us drink the water and wash our eyes and face with it. She never told us what it was all about except that the water held magic. Sometimes, she held her hand over a glass of water and sat for a few minutes with her eyes closed. She said that she was talking to the water and asking the water to purify her body and give her power. Since I was a child, all these rituals were strange and funny.

Nowadays, many articles and conversations talk about "water memory." Can water react to our words, emotions, and vibes? I don't know. I'm not a scholar, but I think for my grandmother and others who believe in the power of water, it gives them a cure, power, and rejuvenation. Each of us needs to have something to believe, something that brings us comfort, good luck, and power to stand on the ground and carry on.

I have used this water method to cure my children as well. While other children were given Tylenol, I helped mine with water. Since I didn't have silent water, I used regular, pure water. I lit a match, made three crosses, told those bad guys to go into the woods, and dropped the match into the water. Then I washed their eyes. Whether or not healing water is due to the power of faith in miracles and skills inherited from my grandmother, the water has always helped my children.

Water has been recognized as an important element for humans and a remedy for diseases by the famous Bulgarian Peter Deunov. He studied medicine in Boston and received a certificate to practice in 1894. His followers called him "Master Beinsa Douno." The name comes from Sanskrit and translates to "He who brings good by word." Deunov himself took up the nickname and used it instead of his own when writing articles. His teachings are still alive and have followers from all over the world.

According to Deunov, water is one of the substances that has the most power on the planet. It's so powerful it can break through stone. Water surrounds us and makes up the largest part of our body. In nature, water cleanses the land. In the same way, it removes impurities from our body.

In Bulgarian folklore, most rituals are performed using water: silent water, colorful water, live water, and holy water. On a number of days throughout the year, called Voditzi or Water Days, you can perform rituals with water. The first is on January 5. At midnight, the sky opens, and you can use water to connect with God and ask Him for protection and health. This is the night where all wishes can come true. Some people use this day to perform magic spells, but I was raised to stay away from both white and black magic. According to my grandmother, magic is an energy that will travel and come back to you, the same with your thoughts.

The next Water Day is the Epiphany, celebrated on January 6. This holiday has various names in different areas of the country, some of them being The Day of the Cross or Water Days. Even though it's cold in January, according to tradition, the priest throws a cross into the river, lake, or other body of water. Men dive in after it. Whoever finds the cross comes out with a smile, despite his frozen body. The silver cross in his hands is like a trophy. It means he'll be healthy and wealthy the entire year.

It's fascinating to see a group of people jumping into the water wearing white clothes. Waves crash against them, and they all look at the priest standing on the sand and holding the cross above his head as he leads the ceremony. The sun shines on the silver cross and sprinkles rays of joy over their heads. It's cold, but the purity and divineness of the moment makes them forget about the weather.

It seems crazy to jump into freezing water, but this is the tradition. Here in America in cities where there's a large population of Bulgarians, you can observe the ritual. In some places, they even dance the horo in the cold river, and the leader of the horo carries the Bulgarian flag. They adopted America as their mother, but still keep the homeland country in their hearts. In the last few years in Chicago, men have performed a horo dance in the icy waters of Lake Michigan, and the young men dive to get the cross from the water for health. In other cities, the tossing of the cross is performed every year.

The last of the Water Days is on January 7. This is the day when young and old, newlyweds and newborns, bathe with the new, baptized water to be healthy and strong all year long.

Water is also important on other days. On the night before St. George's Day (May 6) and Midsummer's Day (June 24), the sick and the healthy bathe in the dew. There's a belief that dew has healing power on these days.

Let's not forget that water is used for baptisms. "Baptism" comes from the Greek word *baptismos*, which means "totally covered with water" or immersed. The early church performed baptisms in rivers, but many times I've witnessed baptisms in the ocean during the summer and even during the winter.

Water, especially "living water," is a subject popular in many songs and tales. The hero needs to find living water and save the princess. According to Bulgarian beliefs and mythology, the only creature that can reach the living water is the eagle.

It heals illnesses and rejuvenates. Take, for example, the Fountain of Youth. People have searched for it and continue to search. Even in America there's a fountain of youth. It's located in St. Augustine, Florida, the oldest town in the country. I was fortunate to visit this city and had a sip of the magical liquid. It's a holy place surrounded by legends.

As we can see, water is a miracle, and we must appreciate it and protect it, so that future generations can enjoy its magical power. Water is needed not only for us, but also for all living creatures and plants.

I'll finish with a quote from Leonardo da Vinci, once called the "Master of the water," who spent a lifetime studying the powerful liquid: "Water is the driving force of all nature."

Chapter 13: Soul of the Bread

I spent most of my childhood time with my maternal grandmother and grandfather, as well as my paternal grandparents, because my parents worked full time in Sofia, Bulgaria's capital, which was a hundred miles away. They didn't have the ability to care for me there. I loved my grandparents, but I missed my parents. They visited during the weekend, not each weekend, but at least twice per month. Sunday evening brought sadness; it was the time I hugged my parents and, standing next to my grandmother on the road, I waved until their car disappeared into the darkness. I hugged my doll and wiped my tears with her curly silver-blond hair. Some days I sat for hours on the fence, hugging my doll and waiting to see the car coming back.

Spending time in the village was a learning experience. My maternal grandparents lived in the same village with my paternal grandparents, but their house was outside in the skirt of the mountain, while my father's parents ran the khan (inn) in the center of the village. My grandmother had to walk two miles to the center of the village where she could get products like sugar, oil, shoes, clothes, and always sweets for me.

They had livestock and produced cheese, milk, butter, eggs, and meat. Every year after they harvested, villagers gathered in the evening for a *sedianka*. It was hosted from house to house: once everyone finished the tasks with one family, the following night the sedianka was hosted at the next house. People sat in a circle husking and spoiling the corn. This involved removing kernels from the cob with a special implement that looked like a metal comb. While holding it in your hand, you twisted an uncooked ear of corn through the opening, grating the kernels off.

Everyone sang and told jokes. It was like a party, but a productive one. It was nice to see everyone having a good time, chatting, eating, and working.

Traditionally, after corn ripens and has been ground, the flour is stored in a dry place and used during the winter to make *kachamak*, a traditional Bulgarian dish. In various regions of the country, it's made differently: some places with milk, others with layers of fried pork, butter, and cheese.

From time to time, I've made kachamak, but no one in my family seems to like it. For me, it's a comfort food bringing back good memories. It's easy to make: you need a pot, water, cornmeal, and salt. Pour the cornmeal over the water. Once it starts boiling, make a hole in the middle of the corn pile. Start mixing the corn with the water until it looks like soft dough. To make sure it's baked well, you need to continue to stir until the mixture starts coming off the pan. Spread one layer on the bottom of a glass pan or any other baking pan, cover it with feta cheese crumbs and butter, make a second layer, and repeat. It's like a cake, but a salty, healthy one.

Baba made it like Bread, and sometime she layered it with a little feta cheese, butter, and red pepper. She said Bread had a soul. *Dobra dusha*, kind soul, is Bread without yeast that's baked in a *podnitza*, an earthenware vessel. To her, it deserved the status of a proper noun: "Bread." She never let me cut the Bread; we had to break it into pieces. She never even allowed me to throw Bread into the garbage; she gathered the crumbs from the table with care and gave them to the dog or the hens.

She separated the yellow corn for the animals and put it in a large wicker basket in the yard. The white corn was reserved for flour. There was also a special corn for popping. We made it on the stove and poured homemade butter over it. It was a tradition we children looked forward to.

White corn was also boiled in winter as a dessert cooked with sugar and walnuts, which my grandmother had roasted with salt in the oven. She gathered the nuts and leaves from a huge walnut tree in the backyard. The leaves helped keep away moths and were a natural dye coloring for yarn and Easter eggs.

From the fresh white corn, my grandparents made flour at Grandpa Stoyan's mill. It was near the village next to a spring called Izvora and a small creek that had enough power to move the mill's stone wheels. Nearby was also the village *kazan*, an important place where people made rakia, a popular homemade brandy made from fermented plums and the remnants of wine at the bottom of barrels.

The mill is still standing, but it's deserted; only the *samodivi* (woodland nymphs) grind flour there, and the *karakondjuli* (night spirits) walk around it in the evening. In the Balkans and in villages, people believe in vampires, karakondjuli, and other evil forces. They perform a ritual to chase them away by swallowing Bread and honey and saying, "Sickness and all evil spirits go into the Thillail forests and never return."

This is a metaphor for a dark place at the end of the world, where nobody wants to go.

Another ritual was to give honey and honey Bread to the samodivi when someone got sick, in the hope that the nymphs would take away the disease. Also, when a hen laid an egg without a shell or one with a soft shell, Baba placed the egg at the center of the crossroads and then asked the spirits for the health of the house by making a special ritual Bread. Since this is in a small village, the crossroad is not a busy place: only a car or two passed by in one week. I always wondered if the egg was still there. I would visit the next day and, seeing no egg, believed the samodivi had taken it. Now thinking about this, I'm sure hungry crows and foxes waited to snatch the easy meal.

On a more spiritual nature, Bulgarians are welcomed to this world with Bread at birth and sent to their eternity with Bread when they die. Bread in the holy church liturgy is a symbol of the body of Christ, and the wine is His blood. We accept it as Holy Communion, which leads to the renewal of life. Ritual Bread is also made for all kinds of occasions: weddings, christenings, funerals, memorials, Christmas, and New Year's. In Bulgaria, at celebrations, every guest is traditionally welcomed with Bread and salt. This is even a tradition that is used during diplomatic visits in Bulgaria.

Ritual Bread is called pitka, and it's round. I always wondered why it had that shape. Baba didn't go to college, but she answered our questions as she saw the world and understood it in her own way. So, according to her, Bread is round because the Earth and the sun are round, and Bread is a symbol of the Cosmos.

The decorations on Bread vary depending on the holiday and the location. People decorate them with flowers, crosses, sun rays, or animals. On pitka, people form symbols of abundance, health, fertility, and happy life. Bread as a symbol is associated with the eternal cycle of life, with infinity, with the circle, with the solar disk, and with the home hearth. Today, pitka is still round, but it doesn't have the same decorations as years ago.

Wedding Bread is called a *zasiavka*. It's basically two types: sweet pitka and *kumov kravai*. Sweet pitka is a loaf of Bread with modest or no decorations. Kumov kravai is, however, rich in decorations, loaded with symbolisms that have a magical effect on the young family. Most often, it includes a bird's image, a symbol of the family.

Another occasion when it's customary to bake Bread and invite people to your house is when a child starts to walk. Along with the Bread, parents select objects like a pencil, book, scissors, and calculator and arrange them on the floor on a white cloth. They toast and roll the round Bread in front of the child and encourage the toddler to walk after it. Once the child reaches the Bread, he or she will become interested in the objects on the cloth and choose one, which determines what occupation the child is fated to be interested in as an adult. If it's the scissors, the child will become a tailor or a hairdresser. Last year, my kids went to an event at the house of an Armenian friend here in Boston where they performed a similar ritual.

Both abroad and in Bulgaria, Bread is a tribute and respected. It's available at all community gatherings. During holidays, it has a central place at the festive table. A few weeks ago, I had the honor of attending a wedding. The groom was a Bulgarian-born American, and the bride was a native-born American. I baked a loaf of Bread to bring, and another lady made a delicious pitka. Everyone stormed to the table where the Bread was.

Sitting at our table were a few guests from the bride's side. They looked at the Bread but weren't sure how to take a piece. "It looks yummy. Do you know how to cut it?" one girl asked. I told her use your hands and broke a piece to demonstrate. "Bulgarians don't use a knife to cut ritual Bread," I added, "because it has a soul." She looked at me as if I was crazy, but finally took a piece. After a few minutes, she broke off a second piece. Others around her followed her example. Later, I saw her dancing the horo.

It takes time to learn a culture, but this is the beauty of discovery and the mixing of people from different backgrounds.

Since Bread is so important, there are a lot of tales and books about it. Baba told us a story about Bread when she removed it from the hearth or the wood stove. We inhaled the sweet smell and watched the brown crust with watering mouths as she explained that the loaf had to go around the fields before we could eat it. We sat and waited. I looked in secret to see if the pitka came back and wondered how the Bread would go to visit the fields since it didn't have legs.

In about an hour, she put the Bread on the table, gently unwrapping the cotton cloth that surrounded it. We greedily eyed the delicious pitka. The crust melted in my mouth when I took a bite. It was the most delicious Bread I've ever tasted, just plain Bread and Bulgarian savory salt. Life in the village was simple, but full of enthusiasm, emotions, and joy for little things.

My grandmother made a special ritual Bread called paraklis, which she decorated with flowers. It's made after the wheat has been harvested and the grain is being crushed. Once the Bread is ready, the oldest woman in the house performs a cleansing ritual of the table with incense. Afterwards, the women go to the nearby cheshma (fountain at a well or spring) where they sprinkle the Bread with water and dedicate it to God to ensure He will help villagers and protect the wheat. The person who breaks the Bread must have a parent still living, so in many cases, this ritual is performed by boys and girls, rather than adults.

The purifying of the table, the Bread, and the house with incense is a widespread rite. It cleanses and gives holiness to the feast. I still use frankincense today to purify our table on special holidays, name days, or feasts and cleanse our home from evil forces. My children always say the house smells like a church.

On Christmas Eve, my family makes round Bread called *bogovitza*, named after the Young God. (In ancient days, *Mlada Boga* or Young God referred to the Sun god. On the winter solstice, he was reborn and his light began to grow longer once again.) After we've finished dinner, we leave everything on the table. I grew up being told that the Young God and our deceased relatives come to the house to eat. I continue to keep this tradition, hoping that the spirit of my dad comes at Christmas and tastes the meals and wine on the table in my home. I'm sure he sees my children and returns happy, somewhere, into the eternal realm.

Even after thirty years, I've kept the memories of my dad; he wasn't only a father but a good friend. My father respected my grandparents, saying that the Old People need to always be near us because they provide wisdom during difficult times.

For ritual Breads, my grandmother used the best white flour, which she sifted three times. She put the flour and yeast or baking soda into a *noshtvie* (a wooden vessel that looks like a trough) and mixed it with silent water or fresh water from the spring.

Sometimes instead, she'd use live *kvas*, a fermented mixture of flour, salt, and water, like a starter dough. A live starter dough lacks bulking agents, enhancers, and preservatives. Therefore, the flour should be clean, pure from the mill, without any enhancers.

When my grandmother was done, she would clean the noshtvie with a small metal spatula with a long handle. The cleaning was an essential part of the baking; it was a ritual for her. On Gergyovden (St. George's Day), she decorated the wooden vessel with greenery, zdravetz (Bulgarian geraniums), so they could give a life force to the Bread and make sure there was always Bread in the house. If a pet jumped over the noshtvie, it was believed that the household would suffer great misfortune.

The noshtvie was passed down from generation to generation. Baba's mother-in-law gave her one. It was a great honor for a bride to inherit it. Just like the Bread that is prepared in the noshtvie, this item itself has a special place in Bulgarian homes. Today you can find them only in antique shops or in villages where life is still preserved in the old ways.

Bread is important not only in the Bulgarian lifestyle, but also in other cultures and is connected with traditions and rituals. Years ago, a colleague gave me Amish friendship Bread. Like kvas, this is the chain letter of baking. The person who makes the starter, similar to a sweet version of a sourdough starter, keeps some to make a loaf of Bread or other baked items. Then they divide the rest to pass on to friends.

Nowadays, we're so attached to our phones and big TV screens that it's unthinkable to take ten days to create a starter before baking Bread. But I think there's a lot of wisdom behind the ritual. It teaches us the importance of simple things. As we keep the starter alive and pass it from one house to another, it unites us and reflects the commonality among us. It was maybe fifteen or more years ago when my colleague gave me the plastic bag with the starter. She made me feel that I was equal to all other people, a friend, and a part of a great team.

I also tried a delicious recipe from my Finnish friend. She's a great baker and the Bread wasn't a disappointment. They call the sweet Bread "nisu." When I made it, it looked like our kozunak: fluffy, yarn-like with a caramelized crust. I guess each culture has its own variety of Bread and rituals devoted to Bread. They all created them because our ancestors needed to survive. They prayed for health and their crops to be protected, to ensure they had enough Bread on the table to feed their families.

There's nothing more delicious than Bread. It's as important as water, and so it's cherished by all cultures. Bulgarian people say no one is bigger than Bread.

There are many other beliefs about Bread. If you touch it with unwashed hands, Bread will blind you. You never cut Bread; you break it using both hands. You never put Bread upside down. My grandmother told me this will bring hunger and illness.

Bread is sacred to the Bulgarians, and must be treated with respect.

Chapter 14: Healers of the Soul

"Do good and throw it on the road—it will catch you sooner or later. Do bad and throw it on the road—it will come again your way."
—Unknown

I don't deny the good of modern medicine. But before we reach out to consume antidepressants and painkillers, we can try to heal with laughter and gifts from nature. Remember the remedies our grandparents and mothers used? Many of them do work.

I've tried to raise and educate my children with this knowledge. When they were small, they asked me many times for pills for pain. But how can you give a child pills for a migraine, ADHD, distraction, or depression? I was a child, and I was distracted, but I never took a pill for it.

It's hard to be in school for eight hours, then have ballet practice and soccer, and have no time to be a child and dream. This is why kids have a hard time concentrating. From daydreams and fantasy, ideas and progress are born. We have to give children their childhood. Pure air, friendships, sports, and books treat and keep our body and soul healthy.

In the past, and even now in Bulgaria, *znahari* exist, people who use herbs, prayers, rituals, divination, and spells or charms to treat and heal others. I call them folk healers. They treat the soul *and* the body. They give people hope for a better future, healing potions for the body, and a prayer for health. They are people whom the locals fear and respect because they must resort to requesting the znahar's help to cure illness or remove fear, stress, and uroki, the latter which you'll know as "the evil eye."

Traditionally, becoming a healer is a practice passed by the female blood line within a close family circle: from mother to daughter, grandmother to granddaughter, aunt to niece. The person who wants to become a healer should have a desire to help people and believe in God, or be a religious and holy person.

In the middle of the summer on June 24, Midsummer's Day or Eniovden, healers and wizards gather herbs before sunrise. My grandmother said every illness had a cure, which is reflected in the seventy-seven and a half herbs of Bulgarian beliefs, each herb being able to cure a specific disease. The half herb is designated for any unknown illness.

Each healer has a magic garden where she gathers the herbs before dawn. Baba was not a healer, but she knew how to collect, preserve, and use herbs. Some she used for cooking and others for healing. She knew how to cure a wound with a leaf of sage, cure upset stomach with tea made from handpicked St. John's Wort. From her herbs, she made different tea blends, such as an aromatic one from thyme, yarrow, and linden. She also blended several herbs to make aromatic spices like the famous *sharena sol*, colorful salt (a mixture of herbs, red pepper, and salt). Warm bread smeared with butter and sprinkled with colorful salt is a mouth-watering, healthy afternoon snack, accompanied by thyme tea and fresh honey.

Besides herbs, znahari use spells or sacred words (often called prayer) for the healing treatment. Their belief in God and their faith give them strength to fight negative energy and cure sickness from fear, stress, and the evil eye. This is a kind of white magic, and the reason many people think they are witches or wizards.

But they don't practice magic; they treat the soul and the body with a suggestion, such as illnesses caused by fear or the evil eye. Everyone has had a moment in their lives when they were scared. My grandmother wasn't a healer, but treated us for the evil eye with water and live coals. If you've watched *My Big Fat Greek Wedding*, you probably remember the scene in the church when the girl's relatives spit on the bride. This is a widespread ritual, a gesture in the Balkans. It's believed to protect people against the evil eye. Also, they can use an amulet, a glass blue eye, "eye of Nazar." It's believed that blue-eyed people have evil power and can make you sick and suck out your energy.

As a child, I remember my grandmother and my mother making an invisible cross on my forehead before I went out somewhere and saying, "Who sees this cross can put a bad curse on my child." Anyone who could see the invisible cross had the ability to harm me, but this same invisible cross protected me from those people. Despite this spell and the red thread sewn into my clothes, sometimes my head ached from fatigue—maybe from the heat or the crowd of women around me, their hugs, kisses, and pats on my cheeks.

In such cases, my grandmother said the evil eye had charmed me. She took a bowl of water and said a little prayer. She opened the metal door of the kitchen stove, removed a live coal from inside, made a cross over a clay bowl, and put the coal into the water as she continued to speak sacred words. If the coal made a noise and broke into pieces, then I was cursed by the evil eye. If it fell to the bottom, the bad energies were absorbed in my bones.

After the ritual, I sipped the water and washed my face. She put a bouquet of herbs, a yellow flower with a sharp smell, maybe oregano, under my pillows to avoid bad dreams and to keep evil forces, dragons, and serpents far away in Zmeykovo (the place where all mythical creatures live).

Unfortunately, I never asked my grandmother for the sacred words of this ritual. I was in America when she died at the age of ninety-nine. She spent her last days with my aunt. Whether she had passed on her knowledge to my cousins, and whether they had embraced her wisdom, I don't know. Nothing was written in a book or on paper, and for many years we lost contact. One of my cousins left this world suddenly, and my aunt followed her to the other world in a few days. Maybe they all are reunited now with my father.

When I was a child, one of my cousins was always afraid. Because of this "sickness," my grandmother took us to a neighboring village to see a znahar who was curing people of fear, depression, and neuroses with a ritual called "cast a bullet." This is an ancient ritual that's alive and widespread even today in different regions of Bulgaria. If someone is afraid, experiencing something that interferes with them carrying on their life, they must have a cast bullet within the first forty days after they get sick in order to drive away the fear so they can heal.

During the ritual, the znahar recites sacred words, the prayer transferred over the centuries from one female family member to the next. No one ever writes them on paper. The prayer is sacred, and each znahar keeps them secret until she's initiated her replacement. Legends say if anyone shares the words or recites the prayers in front of anyone outside of a healing rite, she will lose her healing power.

I expected to see a mystical woman like the sorcerers in the Grimm Brothers fairy tales, but when the door opened, a smiling rural woman, around my grandmother's age, stood there. She invited us into her home and took us into the kitchen, where these kinds of rituals take place. The znahar's wood stove warmed the room and made it cozy. It appeared to relax and reassure my cousin, even though she clenched my hand nervously.

For the ritual, only a few simple things are required: lead, a metal melting pot, a stove, and a clay bowl of cold water. The word bullet frightened us both, but Baba said it was just a word, and it wasn't a real bullet.

The woman put my cousin on a wooden chair and covered her head with a white cloth.

"Don't lie! Don't hate people or beings! Don't steal!" the znahar said.

Baba told me the prayer was to the Virgin Mary. The ritual was simple, and everyone could learn and perform it, but this was just the mechanical part; not everyone can heal people, only those who are dedicated and believe.

She took a metal bowl with a wooden handle, put in a piece of lead, and placed the bowl inside the stove over the hot coals so the lead would melt.

"Don't be afraid, child. We'll say a prayer, and we'll expel the evil forces to the Black Forest. This is the lead," she said.

The woman removed the metal container from the stove. She held the clay bowl with cold water with her other hand, placed it over my cousin's head, and poured the lead into the cold water. The hot metal scraps in the cold water scattered into the shape of figurines. The znahar repeated the same gesture in front of my cousin's heart and knees. While she poured the lead into the water, she murmured something I couldn't hear, but it was the sacred prayer that helped chase away fear.

She took the white cloth from my cousin's head and gave her three sips from the water used in the ritual. You're probably asking, "Why? How can she have someone drink water with lead?" People must still consider the ritual beneficial since it's been around for over 500 years.

"Let's see what scared the child." The znahar shook the bowl and examined the metal figurines in the water. "I see a big, powerful bird here. The child is worried about her family and parents, but it's not a big fear. It's easy to remove and cure."

She poured some of the water into an empty lemonade bottle and told my grandmother on the way home to find a dog and pour it on the dog's head. She explained that as the dog shook off the water, my sick cousin would get rid of her problems. With the rest of the water, she washed my cousin's face.

Shaking her head, the woman continued to look at the lead pieces. She took them out of the water and wrapped them in a white cloth and handed it to my grandmother, instructing her to put it under my cousin's pillow and have her sleep on the figures for three days. After the third day, we would need to take the lead figures to the river and throw them in, so the fear and sickness would go away as the water traveled. She said if Baba needed to bring my cousin back, it had to be on Wednesday as she cast bullets on Wednesdays, Fridays, and Sundays.

In the evening, my cousin and I unbound the cloth and looked at the lead figures. One looked like a cat, another a bird with wide open wings and sharp nails. Its eyes were fixed on us. Thunder in the ceiling made us put the figures back into the cloth, and we covered our faces in fear.

After the third day, we went to Mala River. Baba made my cousin stand with her back to the river and told her to throw the lead figures into the water with her right hand, then put her hand next to her heart. "Dear child, say what your worries are and thank God for your blessing and healing."

We were children, and we didn't understand these strange rituals. My cousin was confused; she kept silent. Baba grabbed the bundle and threw it into the river. "God, please give good life and health to the sick child."

She took our hands and led us to the house. "Go and don't look back!"

Baba was a small woman, but strong and powerful. We obeyed and followed her home. She had suffered so much, and this made her skin thick. She lived a simple life and didn't think bad about people.

Three days after the ritual, my cousin felt good, magic or not, and we had a wonderful vacation in the village. We chased birds, went fishing in the creek, and caught some crabs that hid there.

I often thought about the lead figures that were on the bottom of the river, but I never dared to look for them, nor did I return to that place. The river carried away the sickness and the secret my cousin harbored.

I haven't been subjected to bullet casting in my life, but many have experienced the miraculous power of this sacred ritual. I've heard from Russian-born friends that there is widespread divination in Russia where they use wax to cure and perform fortune telling. I've used live coals in the past for my kids and myself when one of us had a headache, and I've used incense to cleanse bad energy from the house. Whether it's a miracle or a suggestion, it works better than Tylenol.

The important thing is to be kind, respect people, believe in miracles, and have strong faith. This is what helps to heal the soul and the body.

Chapter 15: Orisia or Choice

Life is a journey, not a destination.

Everyone has his *orisia* or destiny. "As it's on stone, it's not written on the head," says a Bulgarian proverb. Many people believe their fate is predestined, their life predetermined, something they can't change. Therefore, they choose to follow the flow in the course of their life. Indifferent, reconciled, waiting for life. Not provoking it, not setting their life to go toward their dreams or in the direction they want it to go.

Others carefully plan their lives step by step: when to get married, how many kids to have, when to buy a house, where to build their lives, and when to retire. Different people, different fates. Sometimes, however much we try to arrange and change life, it seems as if it's going on a predetermined path or, as Bulgarians say, a destiny predetermined by the *oristnizi*.

Who are these mystical creatures, the oristnizi?

In Bulgarian folklore, they're portrayed as three sisters who visit the home of a newborn during the infant's first hours of life. They circle the child's crib, and each one predicts the child's future. The oristnizi appear in fairy tales and artistic works. Some images show their faces, while in others, they are faceless shadows, wrapped in a cloak.

The ancient Slavs believed that only the mother could hear the wishes of these Fates. If she dared to share what she heard, she could lose her voice.

Folkloric rituals about wellbeing, luck, and health go beyond the oristnizi. These concepts have been entangled in the lives of our ancestors for centuries. The rituals and traditions of the Bulgarians are like their soul, filled with hope for a good future and prosperity. They have many rituals, some dating back from the Thracians, some created during the Ottoman rule to protect the family traditions.

Ritual bread plays an important part in these traditions. For example, at Christmas Eve, Budni vecher, we put fortunes for the new year into a ritual pitka bread. We prepare the same kind of ritual bread for the newborn, but the ritual determines his whole life. At least, that's the idea.

According to my grandmother, the first and oldest Fate predicts death; the second, the illnesses and misfortunes that will accompany a person during life; and the third, the youngest, the person's good fortune. The third one always tries to turn the wheel of luck toward a positive direction.

My grandmother took me to a few rituals where I observed a group of women walking around the baby's crib and giving the infant their gifts and wishes verbally. In my eyes, it was a magical ritual that reminded me of Cinderella. I wasn't sure who was the bad one, since they were all smiling, having a good time, chatting and eating sweets. I kept waiting for the door to open with a bang and see an old woman putting a bad spell over the newborn. But none were bad; they were all nice to the baby and me, giving me sweets and pinching me on the cheek with a smile. "She has grown a lot."

In order to make the oristnizi more merciful in their predictions, Bulgarians believe they should bribe the Fates with food and money. This is the reason why after the baby is born and in his room, the mother needs to leave a pot of honey on the table and a gold coin, wrapped in a white handkerchief, under the pillow. This will keep the Fates happy when they visit the baby at night and make sure they are generous in their wishes and gifts.

When I was a child and visited babies with my mother, besides a coin, she had me leave a thread from my clothes to make sure the baby slept well. Also, families place a red thread on the home's threshold to keep evil spirits away from the newborn.

Generally, after the birth of the child, the mother and baby both need to stay at home for forty days to protect them against evil forces outside. In the past, the mother wasn't allowed to attend church as well because she was considered "unclean."

When I arrived in America, my first job was a waitress. I was speechless when I saw a baby, maybe less than a week old, in the restaurant in a small basket, instead of being kept at home. People passed by looking at the baby and making comments. For certain, everyone loved the little angel. The baby didn't open his eyes; the world was new to the little creature.

Back then, I didn't realize how different many of the beliefs and customs were between my home country and my adopted country. I wasn't used to everything being so fast. I never expected a woman to give birth and go back to work after two weeks. Today, even among Bulgarians, who has the time to follow all these old canons?

It doesn't seem like mothers nowadays have the time to create a connection with their child before placing him into the care of someone else for eight hours every day. This is time lost to enjoy motherhood. I was lucky enough to enjoy time with my children when they were little. I needed to work part time, but I had the opportunity to be with them and watch them grow.

My children were born in Bulgaria, and my mother helped me during the first forty-five days after each birth. She didn't follow all the canons, but she made sure I adhered to some. For example, I couldn't leave the baby's clothes outside on the clothesline after sunset. And I had to give each child a bath every day at a certain time, and a massage with oils.

It was March when my oldest daughter was born, so it wasn't that warm. I wrapped her in a few layers of white cotton cloth to make sure she would grow tall and have a good posture. I was afraid she wouldn't be able to breathe and sleep with so many layers of material. It was a precise ritual I repeated every day for forty days.

Times have changed, and the old canons are not alive anymore. New generations use pumps to produce milk and keep it in the fridge so the nanny or the husband can feed the baby. I understand it's difficult to do things the old way in this fast-paced world, but I think we lost something by not following some of the customs. They were established for a perfectly understandable reason: the child and the mother are weak in the first weeks after childbirth; they need time to build up immunities against germs in the human world. Also, it's important for the two of them to bond. The baby is foreign to the mother, like an alien, especially if it's her first child. It takes time to know what babies like, what their different cries mean. Are they hungry? In pain? Wet? But when they smile at you, it feels like you're on another universe.

In olden times, and even nowadays if you follow the traditions, forty days after the birth, the mother goes to church to be purified so she can step back into the world. After this service is complete, the next ritual is called *pogacha*, which is also the name of a sweet bread. It's an occasion to celebrate the birth of the child, where his relatives wish him good luck and health.

The mother's female friends and the baby's close female relatives are the contemporary version of the oristnizi. During their visit, they make their predictions and greetings. They bring sweet things, like cakes and chocolate candies, to make the baby's life sweet, and provide him with gifts that promise to bring him abundance.

Here are some common greetings you can hear at such gatherings, but each person can create her own custom ones to make sure the baby will be blessed in life.

> Be as solid as granite,
> Be strong, vocal,
> Be cheerful and happy,
> Be very hard working.
> To bring joy to your heart—
> Your little sweet boy!

> A golden girl with a golden heart,
> Golden girl with golden hands—
> Golden girl with golden hair,
> Golden girl with golden dreams.

Every mother wants her child to be healthy, happy, and have good luck in life. The pogacha celebration is the desire to gather positive energy around the child to make sure his life is prosperous and will continue the family's legacy.

As in most Bulgarian rituals, the most important part is the bread, the sacred ritual element present at the table for weddings, baptisms, engagements, and funerals. The bread must be made using pure-white flour, and it needs to be a little sweet. It should be made by the mother herself or by a close relative, a woman who has a living parent. Because the celebration is for a sweet life, the table must have traditional sweets: halva, *locum* (Turkish delight), and honey. Like bread, honey is not only an important food product, but also has been used for healing and rituals for centuries. Besides these mandatory elements, wine and other sweets are placed on the ritual table: cookies, cakes, baked goodies. A feast of sweetness.

Only women are guests. When they arrive, it's customary for them to present the baby a gift and a box of chocolate candy. The guests put coins on a white silk or cotton cloth that covers the ritual round bread and wish for the newborn to grow healthy and happy.

After all the guests have arrived, the mother sits in a chair with the child. The scene is magical. Imagine a picture of the old masters: Madonna with a hopeful and happy face and the little angel in her arms, as if she's ready to protect her child all of his life and make his destiny good at all costs. Unconditional mother's love.

Two single girls who have two living parents should break the pitka ritual bread into two pieces over the head of the mother. Regarding the first piece they say, "This is for the Virgin Mary." She will protect and guide the baby in his life path and growth. About the second piece, they say, "This is for the child." His blessing will be to be rich, nourished, and healthy.

After that, they put the bread on the table, and everyone breaks off a piece. The oristnizi immerse it into honey and eat it so the child's life will be sweet and successful. If the crumbs that fall are small, the next child will be a girl. If they are bigger pieces, the baby will be a boy.

The mother ties the white cloth and gives it to the eldest woman and tells her to make a wish for the child and then pass it to the woman next to her. The bundle of coins passes from hand to hand until it reaches the mother again, who also pronounces her wishes for the child. She places the coin bucket high in the home, on a shelf so the child grows toward success and spiritual purity.

"Throw the umbilical cord stump away for luck; keep the child going forward" is a popular saying in Bulgaria both in the past and nowadays. A young mother who wants to influence and define a good destiny for her child performs this ritual, but creates new variations.

It's believed that if you place the stump in the garden and plant a tree on it, the child will grow strong and will have the strength and power of the tree. It also creates an anchor and connects the child to his roots. Other mothers place the stump in the house to keep the child close to them. I've heard that parents insert the stump into a book or leave it in a school or university so the child becomes a scholar.

I've read that the Native American Navajos bury a newborn's umbilical cord, sealing their relationship with the earth. In Africa, when a baby is stillborn (or as they say, "it is late"), they bury the umbilical cord along with the afterbirth with the child to keep the infant's spirit at rest.

In recent years, people preserve the cord for future medical use. According to recent research, cord blood has been shown to contain stem cells that can be used for life-saving stem cell transplants for children and adults.

Interestingly, I preserved the tradition of placing the stump somewhere after I gave birth. When you have your first child, everything is exciting and new. You learn and have great hopes and wishes for the prosperity of your child.

My uncle agreed on one of his trips to Switzerland to take my older daughter's stump and leave it in a bank. In my mind, this was the country and the place to provide her with success and stability. Unfortunately, my younger daughter's stump was lost and stayed in the hospital where she was born. It's in the hands of fate maybe because she's taken the path of medicine. Fate or chance?

Both girls learn and work hard, build their lives, and determine their fate every day. Parents only give their children an opportunity to develop. The children themselves must determine their own destiny and professional path.

The sweet bread ritual is just the beginning of a series of rituals to call forth good fortune and luck. A child saying his first word and taking his first step are important and memorable moments for parents and relatives, not only for Bulgarians but for all parents. For Bulgarians, this is yet another reason to challenge fate and turn it down a predestined path. This time there are no oristnitzi, but it's the bread that guides the child in the dawn of his life. The ritual is called *prostupulnik* and is performed after the child has taken his first steps. Again, the bread is the center of the celebration. It needs to be round and not decorated. It must be made and baked by a woman with living parents in order to protect the child from evil forces.

In some areas of the country, the family places the bread on a chair or a small round table and scatters objects around it on the ground on a white cloth. I came from northern Bulgaria. There, the mother rolls the bread on a white canvas cloth covered with objects. Every object has a certain meaning. After the bread rolls, the child steps toward the white cloth and chooses an object. Whatever he chooses signifies what his profession will be. If the child takes a comb, he'll be a hairdresser; if he takes a book, a teacher; a brush, an artist; and so on. Before, the objects were simple: ladle, spindle, scissors, book, stethoscope, and more to predict the child's profession or calling. Nowadays, parents choose and use objects from the modern way of life.

The mother then breaks the bread and gives it to the guests. In the past, the custom required the mother to run to three neighboring families with the pieces of bread. While running, she tried not to stumble so the child wouldn't stumble in life. But this is no longer practiced, especially here abroad, where we often don't know our neighbors, even though we've lived next to them for years. I imagine how Miss Anderson next door will look at me if I give her a piece of bread dipped in honey and say she needs to eat it to make sure my daughter will become a surgeon.

These customs have been practiced from ancient times, handed down from mother to daughter, with the idea of preserving family traditions and defining a better life for our children.

Mankind from ancient ages has been trying to mold and define its future, see or predict what's going to happen. But is our future a repetition of our past? Is our life destined as the Bulgarian commandment says: what is written on stone will happen? Can we change our fate?

Chapter 16: Skinny Tulips

"To paint is to love again."
—Henry Miller

Silence is interrupted by the rumbling of pencils, the squeaking of erasers, and the soft footsteps of a lady who walks around the tables, watching each student. I hold my breath, look at the colorful tulip bouquet at the front of the room. The sun glitters against droplets of water on the glass jar.

I never thought I'd get admitted to the prestigious Sofia Art school exams. Me, a girl from a village, who grew up in a family of people who think a poster is a painting. But in life, if you don't try, you'll never know whether you'll succeed or not.

That morning when I left home, my mother spilled a bucket a water in front of me for good luck. My father hugged me and sent me away with a proud look on his face. I was in a hurry, nervous, and didn't say anything to him. He was a man of many talents and most of all an ability for appreciating life. If I'd have known he would pass away in a few months, I would have spent more time with him, appreciated his goodness more. Life has its own way of surprising us. Even if we carefully plan each of our steps, sometimes it's hard to win or know which path or action to take until it's too late.

That day, the only path I could think about was taking the art exam. It was my chance to demonstrate what I could do.

I got off the train at the "Pope" plaza, with the Patriarch Evtimiy Monument welcoming me. Holding on tight to a folder and a few pencils, I headed toward the Art School building. Most of the applicants who were here to take the exam had descended from intellectuals and families of renowned artists. They had arrived with teachers, parents, and supporters, and stood off aloof, away from me.

I was nervous and felt like a black sheep, out of my league. I didn't have the training and resources like the other students, nor had I taken drawing lessons like them, but I had participated in the international Peace Flag Assemblies and won awards. That gave me a little confidence, because only gifted children had been chosen to participate.

As I climbed the narrow, dark staircase, the smell of oil paint engulfed me. I felt as if I were entering a temple of art. I took my seat and waited. The exam was to draw the tulips in the glass jar at the front of the room.

The clock on the wall in the exam room measured the seconds, the minutes. I felt sweaty, boiling under the heat of the day. I wanted to demonstrate my talent and passion, but my hand felt paralyzed.

The girl next to me looked at my drawing and shook her blond curls with a sorry smile. I looked around helplessly. Everyone was focused, measuring the flower proportions with pencils, catching the shadows, and working on their paintings with trained strokes. I wondered if I should leave.

No, I was there to stay and show what I could do. I didn't want to give up that easily.

I looked around again. No, not everyone was focused. The boy in the first row got a glass of water and took a valium. The girl next to him opened a box of expensive pencils and examined her beautiful manicures; she sharpened pencil after pencil, looking around to see if anyone was paying attention to her.

I tried to ignore what the others were doing, recalling words of advice from one of my teachers: "Draw what you see. Don't look at the others. Everyone sees the world differently. Don't copy anyone. Be yourself even if it's difficult!"

My hands were shaking. I tried to grasp the volume, the perspective, the shape, but everything changed. The tulips that were buds at the beginning of the exam were now in full bloom, dancing under the warm rays of the sun. "Be yourself. This is your worldview." I repeated my words of courage.

The clock struck noon, and the exam was over. I looked at my skinny tulips and compared them to the ones the girl next to me drew. Hers had trained strokes; the lines, the lights, the shadows all showed finesse. A perfect composition.

I looked at my drawing and saw my grandmother's garden tulips: crazy, imperfect, dyed by the sun, crushed by the Balkan wind. Art is not only about how you control your hands to draw the strokes; to be a good artist, you must speak to your audience. If your art creates emotions, takes the person who is observing the painting to a different world or brings back memories, happy or sad, then you can call yourself an artist.

Even today, when I visit Bulgaria and walk past the Art School, I think of my bouquet of skinny tulips. Unfortunately, I missed a few points on the exam score and wasn't accepted to the school. Nonetheless, it was an experience that left a mark in my life. It taught me that having a gift or talent isn't enough. You need to work diligently, train your mind and hand if you want to be good. This is true not only for art, but for any profession. I also felt I didn't have the necessary resources and background to succeed in art. Back then, everything was about who you know, the people around you. Maybe I was mistaken, but that's what I thought at the time. I was an outsider, and so I didn't succeed.

Not succeeding doesn't mean failure. I traveled along a different path. I discovered the beauty of wood when I was later accepted in a school to study woodcarving. I was again surrounded by children of famous poets, artists, and people with money to pay for art lessons. This was my second chance, and I proved to be one of the more talented students. I discovered the soul of wood and created beautiful carvings, fashioning my dreams.

I had the opportunity to meet interesting and talented people and make new friends. A class of young, crazy, talented people, lost and looking for themselves. We all had ideas and dreamed of what we were going to do. Due to changes in Bulgaria and other events, we moved in different directions, scattering around the world and never connecting again. I would love to meet my school friends and acquaintances again, finish the story of what happened in our lives. I wonder what other chapters they wrote, where they all went, and what they did with their lives.

I was at school when my father died. My world crashed, something burst inside me, and my life changed.

Some people are good coping with loss. I'm not one of them. I was so upset and sad, and it took a toll on my school and art career. After graduation, I wasn't able to find work in the field. Back then, this was a man's profession. So I quietly found a job with which I could support myself financially.

The itch for art never went away. It's like old love; it stays with you. Now, in my fifties, even though it's late in life, I want to start again. I can do it, I know. I still have the talent and the creative flame buried within me.

When we cannot fulfill our dream, it remains forever in us as a seed waiting for the right moment to grow and sprout. Years passed, and life took me to distant countries, but that love and desire to create traveled with me. Hidden somewhere deep inside me. I captured every moment, every object and experience around me. Life experience, obstacles, and love are the best ways for an artist, writer, any kind of creator to discover himself.

I was a sick child and traveled from school to school all over Bulgaria. For some, this will sound sad. It was sad and difficult for me because I lacked a mother's caress, the family hearth. On the other hand, it was an opportunity to discover many places in Bulgaria, meet interesting people, get to know their customs and culture. Bulgaria is a small country, but its culture is like a multicolored rug. Each region has its charms, history, dialects, dances, and folklore. Everywhere, people are the same; they love to share their meals with you; give you the best bread, food, wine, and rakia brandy; and welcome and respect you. In return, they desire our respect and a simple thanks, nothing more.

Once you break away from your home, you become a wanderer, wander like a child and discover everything in the world around you. I left my home as a young child and my experience, my travels and encounter with different people and cultures are what shaped me as a person and artist. This life experience reflects in my art. It's vivid and diverse, nostalgic sometimes, inspired by my roots, always surprising and filled with imagination.

Chapter 17: The Soul of a Tree

Have you ever wondered if trees have souls?

If you stand within a tree's shade, try pressing yourself to its bark to feel its heart pulsing and its leaves rustling like a whisper. Think about a centuries-old tree falling to the ground. The thunder is heard for hundreds of feet. Like a defeated giant after a long and heavy battle, the tree's body relaxes on the ground. Even though the tree itself has been destroyed, new shoots of sun-drenched branches emerge from its roots. It continues to grow as long as its roots are not extracted from the ground.

As a child, I imagined every tree as a person. The old walnut was a white-bearded old man with a wrinkled face; the pear was a huggable grandmother with her arms outstretched; the quince looked like a magnificent, smiling aunt; the willow danced like a ballerina to the whistling of the wind.

Trees are all around us. They are the lungs of the planet, filtering the air. In summer, they provide us cool shade from a sometimes-brutal sun. We enjoy their blossoms in spring and their beautiful colors in autumn. In winter we enjoy warmth from their wood in the fireplace. We use wooden implements to do housework, and wood to build our houses, schools, churches, iconostasis, art, and other objects used in everyday life.

In America, laws protect nature, ensuring our trees and forests are not completely wiped out. We can't stop all forests from being destroyed for their wood, but the law protects parks and nature reserves.

When we arrived in America twenty years ago, the plane landed in Boston. It was late in the evening and on our way to the home of our friends who would shelter us for the first few days, we saw only lights and silhouettes. The next morning my oldest daughter's laughter woke me. She was standing in her pajamas by the window, pointing outside with eyes wide open. When I looked, I was speechless. Several gray squirrels bounced from branch to branch in the crown of a huge tree covered with golden, orange, and red leaves, like an artist's palette. Some of the leaves had fallen onto a green carpet of well-cut grass. Green, trees, sun. Hypnotized, I went out barefoot and felt the dew on my soles. My daughters followed me. I felt like a child.

Was I dreaming? It felt surreal. It was an experience I will never forget. My first encounter with nature in an American suburb. We were in a town, one of many near Boston, with clean streets, green lawns, shrubs, and trees. Yes, as we saw it in Hollywood movies. But it didn't feel like a city. It was more like living in a remote hut on the top of a mountain.

After twenty years in America, I'm used to seeing greenery and trees. Large oaks surround our house and provide shade in summer and protection from the chilly winds in winter. In autumn, the leaves fall, and we complain that we need to collect them in sacks, but working outside helps us get closer to nature.

I love the whisper of the willows. We planted two beautiful weeping willows next to each other, like two sisters, reminding me of my children. Believe it or not, I grew them from two little shoots that I cut off the tree at my girls' school bus stop. The trees are more than twenty years old, growing up before our eyes in the same way our children did.

We planted a fir tree, and every Christmas we decorate it with lights. Santa Claus leaves presents there overnight year after year. The fir tree is already large, and every needle on the branches has recorded our beautiful memories.

In Bulgaria, my grandfather invested his money in land and forests. After 1941, the Communist Party confiscated all his estates and destroyed the forests without his permission. The division and distribution of forests is still a burning topic, and people continue to be killed for property. Unfortunately, the destruction of forests in Bulgaria continues today without planting new ones to replace them.

Everything in nature has its place. The destruction of forests affects not only bees, birds, and all its inhabitants, but also the waters. The network of tree roots protects riverbanks like natural levees. It's no wonder floods and mudslides dump houses and people down cliffs when trees along the rivers have all been chopped down.

Years ago in Sofia, chestnut trees lined the middle of the streets and the parks. The scent of white flowers filled the capital, and the greenery cooled the asphalt from the burning rays of the summer sun. Golden leaves covered the streets during autumn. Over the years, the city grew, the number of cars increased, streets widened, and the chestnuts lost the fight against asphalt. The last time I visited my mother, I heard that illness and small parasites threatened to destroy the surviving chestnuts. And other trees could be ruined as well if the disease continues to spread and no one cares about the green areas of the city. Asphalt, cars, and dust cover the narrow streets instead of the beauty of trees.

They say you need a whole village to raise a child, but the same can be said of a tree. It's hard to grow a tree. It's like a human. It needs to find the right place and the correct soil to grow healthy and happy.

I read an article about palm trees in Ecuador that are moving to find light, water, and good soil. They grow new roots that reach the water and let the old die allowing them to move and reach good soil and light. Interesting, right? This is like humans. We're looking for a better life and livelihood, and so we travel, we wander, from place to place.

Unfortunately, the destruction of forests isn't a phenomenon only in Bulgaria; it happens all over the world. I'm glad when I see news about people planting trees, trying to recover the destroyed treasure and help the planet breathe.

The most common mythical symbol of the universe is the "World Tree." Its separate parts symbolize the three layers of the world. The crown symbolizes the heavens—God, the saints, and the angels live there. The stem represents earthly life, and the roots the underworld. The tree is woven as a motif in Bulgarian rug patterns, embroidery, and wedding rituals.

The tree for many people and nations is a symbol of the connection between the earth and the sky. With roots deep in the soil and branches bending toward the sun. Almost all the ancient nations worshiped the tree—real or idealized. It was attributed to the cosmic symbols. According to ancient religions, trees are living creatures; they're inhabited by spirits of nature, nymphs, and elves. Every tree has its own soul. And every tree has its owner or dragon (zmey).

Sacred places in villages called *obroks* are scattered under branches of centuries-old trees. They're found near springs, places where the whole village gathers to celebrate, perform sacrifices, and honor the soul of the tree. The centuries-old trees and obrok require special tribute, in the same way chapels, churches, and monasteries do. People believe that praying to the tree and the creature within it will keep the village safe from evil forces and will bring fertility and prosperity to the land and people. Normally in these sacred places, you see stone slabs or stone crosses. Sometimes people drill holes in the tree, pour in oil and other offerings, and cover the hole with wax to feed the spirits.

In my grandparents' village, there are several old obroks. One of them is for St. George. It's at the highest and most beautiful part of the village. The church was built near the obrok in the early twentieth century. Both are places for the villagers to pay respect to the saint.

These sacred places are created under oak, beech, and other centuries-old trees. Bulgarians usually think of oak, maple, walnut, and pine as World Trees. The mythology of the mountain people retains pre-Christian beliefs, according to which the world is a great oak tree. The image of an oak and an eagle on the top is a prototype of the World Tree and is found in legends, tales, and stories and in traditional songs of the people of northern Bulgaria, where my ancestors are from. This image also occurs on iconostasis carvings and thrones in the churches. These eagles are believed to be the guardians against hail, and they protect fields from fire and lamia, an evil dragon. The oak is also a road between the upper and the lower land, our world and the underworld.

Tradition has strictly forbidden people from even chopping their branches. The old ones believe that if you cut down such a tree, you and your family will be cursed, and you'll get sick and die because a saint is sitting inside it.

It sounds ridiculous, but I think my father who left this world suddenly at an early age may have broken this rule and paid with his life. He cared for his family, worked a lot, had many talents, and built a house, not only one, but a few houses. He was building one for a grandmother whose old home the Communist had destroyed. However, an old walnut, with towering branches and heavily rooted in the ground, proudly sat near the foundation, hindering the construction of the home. On the ninth of September, my father decided to cut it down. I don't remember the year. I think it was 1981 or 1982, but I'm certain it was September 9.

How do I remember the date? On the ninth of September every year, there was music in the center of the village, people commemorating the Communist Party's anniversary. The tree was a few yards from the square, and the mayor came personally to stop the cutting of the tree, because the noise was interfering with the holiday. My father ignored him, and after a few hours, the old giant crashed down.

My father used the walnut wood to make windows, doors, and other things for the new house. The boards had unique patterns and colors. Because of these features of walnut, iconostases in churches are made of this wood. My father continued the construction of the house, but after a couple of years, he died suddenly on his fiftieth birthday, unable to see the completed fruit of his labor. I always think that the saint or the spirit who was living in the walnut tree took his spirit with him. The old walnut's soul is built into the house, and every time I go there, I can feel it.

If trees had voices, think about what they could tell us: what they saw and heard over hundreds of years. In Luti Dol in Bulgaria, my grandmother's village, there's a cheshma and a small creek called Bivola. Nearby is a willow people say is more than 500 years old. I always wondered what the tree saw during those 500 years. Along the spring runs the old road to Sofia. Maybe the tree saw the rise and fall of the Turks, the lines of families rushing to get out to save their lives during the wars.

Gold and treasure gathered from the sweat and misery of the people once was transported over this road. Maybe the tree saw German and Russian soldiers in 1944. Every time I was at the spring with my grandmother, I always touched the tree's trunk in the hope of hearing its voice, waiting to hear its story.

The village has an old legend from 1765 that its inhabitants pass on mouth-to-mouth. One summer morning, a group of youths who were hunting in the woods saw a strange woman on one of the hills around the village. She had a terribly ugly face, a bony body, and long, shaggy hair. She drew a big bow, and with malice began to send blazing arrows toward the village. All the young people who lived there were struck by a terrible disease. The old men in the village gathered together, wondering what this curse was and how to save the people, but it was too late. One of the elders told them that it was Mora, the horrible plague. The disease spread like fire and destroyed almost the entire village. Fear, weeping, and smell of death passed through the empty streets. The people who escaped from the village were overtaken by the arrows of the disease, and hundreds of bodies covered the surrounding meadows and forests near the village. Not many people survived the plague, but those who did were able to rebuild, and the area was named "Dead Meadows" as a reminder of the event and the people who died.

Everyone believes in something that brings hope and peace to their soul. For millennia, people have believed in mythical beings, deities, and holy trees; others believe in the power of crystals. All of this helps us to not fear the uncertainty of life and to predict the course of events in our lives. Our life is like a chapter of a book that has no end. Everyone writes their chapter to leave a trace behind them.

I always wanted to have the ability to talk to trees. I can learn so much from them.

Chapter 18: The Gate – Coffee, Cigarettes, and a Drop of Wine

In memory of my father.

The sky dissolved, and a flood of rain carried houses, fences, barn animals, and graves to the river. My tears merged with the torrent, day and night, night and day, the sorrows like hot coal burned into my soul, until my eyes could weep no more from grief. The day my father died something burst inside me.

Everything and everyone around me reminded me of Dad, the emptiness he left gaping like a pit. Mom and Baba Maria were spinning around the house, hiding their pain. I could tell my brother secretly suffered in his own way. He didn't cry, but I could see the pain in his eyes and his emotional shock. His arms lay limp at his side. He stalked the corner and didn't talk, but his body language was clear that he was in pain as if he was carrying a bag with stones.

My grandmother stroked my head. "Don't worry, my child, and don't cry. It's not good to weep for the dead. Your father will go to a good place. It was his time to leave. The Lord loves him and needed talented people to be around and help him."

"Baba, is it love to take someone away from those who loved him?" My heart was pounding with pain. I had lost a father and a friend.

If you didn't know my grandmother, you'd think she didn't love us. Her face was like stone on the outside, and inside she kept her love and soul hidden behind a wire fence. Roses blossomed there, but it was hard to touch them without a lot of fuss. It kept her strong after she'd sent my grandfather to the other world early, and lost her parents when she was a toddler. But she had a lot of love that she showed us in her own way.

When my father left for the other world, we silently sent him to his eternal life on the hill near the church next to my grandfather Ivan, his father. A few weeks later, someone else in the village died.

My grandmother silently made a package that she tied up in a white cotton cloth: baked bread, cheese, a jar of honey. She picked marigolds and red geraniums to make a bouquet. After removing a box of locum, a common sweet used in rituals, and cookies from the dolly (what you'd probably call a bread box), she headed for the stairs.

"Baba, where are you going with those flowers?" I rushed after her, thinking grief had clouded her mind.

She said she was going to "buy him back," meaning my father. I wondered what she could buy to get him back.

When I asked her what she meant, Baba told me seriously, "He's sitting at the cemetery gate and guarding it."

"Baba, what's he guarding?"

"He's the guardian of the gate. He's waiting for the next person who dies to arrive to take his place. Then your father can continue his journey to his eternal home."

I sobbed again, imagining my father alone on the doorstep, in the rain, wet and cold. Since childhood, my imagination has been vast. I didn't care that my grandmother could "buy him back" by bringing gifts to the family of someone who died after my father. She would ask the deceased person to take my father's place guarding the gate, so that my father could move on. In my eyes, my father was a saint, respected and loved, and he was certainly already in heaven. Back then, there was no talk of Paradise and Hell because church ordinances and beliefs were forbidden. But who can forbid you from believing in good and the souls of people?

My grandmother straightened the black scarf covering her head, took the food package and the fresh flowers, and in small steps walked to the deceased man's home to leave her presents near him during the wake. She lit a candle for the man who had died and sent him greetings and asked that after his traveling that he would take over the post when he met my father at the gate, so my father's soul could be free to go on his heavenly path.

It's a ritual that's done from time immemorial, passed down from mother to daughter. People believe that the soul travels to its favorite places. After forty days on earth, it stays at the gate between the worlds to meet the one who follows it, so the new soul isn't alone, and doesn't get lost.

In northern Bulgaria, it's a custom on souls' day to pour wine over your loved one's grave and when you leave, to pour a drop at the cemetery gate. Some soul always sits there at the invisible doorstep. Wine is poured as a symbol of remembrance for all souls—for those you know and those you've never met. Baba used to carry home-baked bread, boiled wheat with sugar and nuts, and wine when she visited the cemetery to honor all the dead.

My father left without saying goodbye, suddenly passing away in my brother's helpless arms. He left a permanent mark on his heart, like a hot, open wound that's still smoldering after all this time. My brother doesn't share his feelings, but I know he's still suffering and thinking about our father. Death grabbed him and carried him away.

My mother was young, only forty-two, with a life full of hopes and dreams ahead of her. My father had loved her a lot, and she was happy. The house was filled with cheer, friends visited often, my father played music, and they sang around the table. After he died, she continued to care for us even though pain filled her heart. It was hard on us and on her. Her eyes were empty, and the joy was gone, but she comforted me and my brother because she was afraid we would be scared and sad. My mother kept us together, and my brother had to become the man of the house.

People tried to comfort us with hugs and smiles, and their sorrowful looks told us they wanted to help make the hurt go away. But they couldn't, and I wished they would all leave. After a month, our friends and loved ones finally left to return to their world. The house that had been filled with people was empty, the music stopped, and the laughter left our lives. Our friends were gone, and we felt forgotten, but allowed to finally grieve on our own.

One thing I understood was that death brings grief to loved ones, but they continue to live even with heartache. When a person leaves this world, his life is interrupted and lost. He loses the chance to live, to enjoy, to suffer, to see weddings and grandchildren, and to grow old with his companion in life or his family.

Different funerary customs exist throughout Bulgaria, with each region having its own traditions and beliefs. People wear black for mourning and pay homage to the deceased. They print obituaries, with a poem or some saying and the name of the person, and glue them on doors, sign posts, shop billboards, and post offices. If someone doesn't understand the language, they think that the person in the picture is wanted for a crime. This ceremony continues throughout the year, with signs being posted for the forty days the soul is traveling, then again after six months, and again at the year anniversary of the death.

Visiting the grave occurs often, too. My mother didn't smoke, but when she visited my father at the cemetery, she lit his favorite cigarettes and put on his grave a cup of his favorite coffee and a vase of fresh flowers from the garden. We share that love of coffee; black coffee without milk or other spices brings me pleasure, the scent of pure joy. He also loved to make and eat butter and honey crepes, which was my favorite Sunday morning breakfast.

It's believed in Bulgarian folklore and customs that after one year of death, the deceased has finally taken his place in the other world and lives among relatives and family ancestors. People no longer burn candles separately in the loved one's memory, but instead honor them by saying prayers for all deceased relatives together.

According to beliefs, Archangel Michael takes the soul of a person when he dies. That's why the archangel is also called the soul taker. One of the biggest days commemorating souls is the Great Day of Souls, which occurs on the Saturday before Arkhangelovden (November 8). It's a day to make sure the memories of the dead live on in the lives of the living. It's reminiscent of the care of the angels of God for the dead, and is specifically dedicated to the fallen warriors, and is also referred to as the "male day of souls."

During this day people visit their loved ones and family members. They share food such as sweets, candy, fruit, boiled chicken, and wine. It's given not only to loved ones, but also to strangers visiting the graves.

In America, we celebrate Memorial Day in May in remembrance of our loved ones, and Veteran's Day in November honors those who have fought for our country. Lesser-known to most is All Soul's Day, which Catholics celebrate on November 2 to pray for souls they believe are in purgatory. At one time, the Church also sold "indulgences," which were a way for people to do penance for sins and thereby reduce their time in purgatory.

In Mexico, people honor those who have gone on before them in a festival called Day of the Dead. It's not filled with mourning and weeping, but bright colors and laughter. Like the Bulgarians, the Mexicans believe in feeding their dead as they travel to the spirit world.

Many other countries have similar traditions to honor their loved ones who are no longer with them. The traditions are different everywhere, but what brings them closer is the idea of honoring and remembering our ancestors and their memory.

Every time I walk past a graveyard, I wonder who sits there at the gate and waits for his shift to end so he can take the eternal path to the beyond.

Chapter 19: Don't Be Late

The outlines of houses and roads disappear in the thick blanket of fluffy white clouds. At 30,000 feet, I drop the back on my seat and close the window cover to prepare for the next seven hours of inactivity during my flight. I open my book, but the lines merge into one.

I'm afraid of the unknown.

Am I too late? Will I be unable to say goodbye to my mother? Chills creep along my back. I grab the blanket and cover myself like a cocoon.

Over the steady noise of the airplane motors, the flight attendant interrupts my thoughts. "Miss, what would you like to drink?"

"Red wine. Please give me two glasses."

With a smile, she hands me a glass and a package of crackers.

My voice sounded desperate, I think.

The warmth of the alcohol relaxes me, and blood flows through my cheeks, but then hunger gnaws at me. I haven't eaten since last night. I open the crackers. They're crisp and melt like an expensive aged cheese in my mouth. The good Italian wine and excellent service help make the trip more pleasant, but they don't wash away my anxieties.

I never thought about this time in my life, but it came, and I'm not prepared. Children grow up and take their own paths in life, but at the same time, parents get old. What makes this worse and more complicated for me and others living abroad is the distance. Our parents need our care and our presence. We have a dilemma about how to take care of them. Thanks to technology, we can see each other on Skype, Facebook, and FaceTime. We send our loved ones our greetings, hugs, and kisses, but we also see the sadness on their faces.

They say that with money you can buy everything, but that doesn't apply to love and care.

In Bulgaria, tradition requires children to care for their aging parents. Like in Asia and some other cultures, in Bulgaria multiple generations live together in one house and take care of the elderly. It's an honor to have the grandparents live in the house. It also creates a connection between generations.

It's a different story in America. Families often place the elderly in nursing homes or assisted-living facilities. It can be prestigious to live at some of these places, which resemble an expensive resort. If you can afford it, it's an excellent place to live, where doctors, nurses, and other staff are available to you twenty-four hours a day. Shuttles take you shopping or to nearby casinos, where you can spend money and have fun. The staff organize activities to cheer you up. More often, however, the elderly end up in places where the staff are underpaid and overworked. They have little time to care for more than the immediate physical needs of the residents. Some of these places have been known to not even provide that much care.

In the past in Bulgaria, if you sent your parents to a nursing home, it was a disgrace for the family. People said you abandoned your parents. My mother spent seven years of her life caring for her parents, who both were confined to their bed and were unable to move or eat by themselves. Seven years of agony and devotion. Is this right or wrong? Is it the best solution for their care? I don't know. Who am I to judge?

One of the Ten Commandments of God is "Honor your father and mother." God wants us to honor our parents. We must respect them, regardless of whether we think they deserve it or not. Love is far less of a commitment than honoring them. But, if we honor our parents, we show our love for them even if they aren't perfect. It means in any situation and in front of everyone, you can, with a sense of pride and respect, say, "These are my parents."

I'm proud of my father, whom I lost more than three decades ago. He was an honest and proud laborer, whom both his friends and children revered. He was a man of many talents and was able to build a life for us and my mother, despite the challenges he and his family faced during the Communist era. Even today, people mention his name with respect.

I'm also proud of my mother, who devoted her life to me and my brother. She gave us a foundation in life, despite how much work it was and how much it deprived her of living her own life. She's not well-known; she's not a star. But she is my mother, a single, quiet, modest woman, who has worked and labored for a lifetime, only to get a pension with which she can buy a weekly basket of groceries. Regretfully, she's not the only one, but I don't want to write about poverty and deprivation in Bulgaria; that's another topic.

In my mind, I see her standing next to my bed, holding my hand and smiling. She cared for me when I was sick, when I was sad, and during those moments when my world was turned upside down. She always took care of her family with tenderness, patience, and love. Since my father died, she's had a difficult role, but she always succeeds in every situation, loving us and protecting us.

I'm jolted back to reality as the landing gear touches ground. I'm back on Bulgarian soil. The woman at the border control tells me something, but I don't hear her. I take back my passport and look for the exit sign and my waiting brother.

His embrace and his calm face are signs that everything is fine with our mother. I'm on time.

On the way to the hospital, I don't know how to break the awkward silence in the car. What should we talk about? I don't know his concerns or worries. I don't know what excites him. Life separated us, and now we're as close as aliens. Our shared memories stopped twenty years ago. His friends and even strangers know more about him than I do.

Even thousands of miles away, I love him; he's my brother. But there's nothing to say because we're separated by the different worlds we live in. We have different friends, interests, and dreams. We have different worries and problems.

At times like this, I wonder if I made a mistake by leaving home and abandoning my relatives, my brother, and my mother. But every person should be free to choose and build his own life. My conscience, like little sharp teeth, bites me and reminds me of my choices every day.

During my years away, I've lost many friends and close relatives without being able to say goodbye. All my life I'll reproach myself for this failing. I can't cry; my tears dried up and my heart became wrapped with thorns the day I lost my father. Maybe that's why I'm a wanderer, a wanderer who's looking to find herself and travels to escape the pain. And now I'm going to face more pain when I see my mother.

The only sound in the car is the roar of the engine. My brother smokes a cigarette while he drives. I hate the cigarettes, but I love him, so I don't want to ask him to throw the butt away. I breathe the smoke and quietly look out the window.

A few years ago, I wanted to surprise my brother for his birthday. My sister-in-law and the rest of the family helped me organize a wonderful celebration. We went to a holy place, high up in the mountain, a monastery where we had good memories with my father and where my children were baptized. His birthday is on June 24, Eniovden or Midsummer's Day, one of my favorite holidays, so it was a double celebration. Everyone held lively conversations around the table, but the event turned cold and sad for me. This was my family, friends, and relatives, but I felt like a stranger sitting at their table.

Words come to my mind, like a slow sad melody. A poem of loss and sorrow.

Unfinished Tales
The envelope is faded and yellow,
A dollar stamp from 1998,
A folded page of tales,
An unfinished letter to my friend.

Shame for not finding the time
To listen, write back and be present,
Continue to be your dear friend,
Even from the other side of the ocean.

Holding the yellowed paper,
Sadness covers my face.
Who is there to blame
For not finding the time
To say the last goodbye?

It is too late for regrets.
Wipe your tears and go
Embrace today and dream for tomorrow.
Finish all other unfinished tales.

My heart beats faster. My brother stops in front of a white luxury building. We're at the hospital. The muddy, overcrowded parking lot drowns out my admiration for the building. With our sandals soaked because of the heavy rain, we find the entrance and rush to the front desk.

The sad face of the woman behind the desk and her inquisitive eyes shake me. Has something worse happened to my mother? I rush away, trying to figure out where to go. Maybe she gave us the wrong floor. Bustling people in blue and white uniforms fly by us everywhere. Finally, we manage to find my mother's room.

She looks tired, but her smiling face makes me forget about everything. It's the same smile I remember from my childhood. I embrace her small, weak body and feel happy.

"Everything will be fine. Your kids are here." I hug her tight.

I am on time.

Author's Note

Three major periods mark the formation and development of Bulgarian communities abroad.

The first occurred at the turn of the twentieth century. More than forty Bulgarian organizations were established in the United States, mainly for educational, cultural, church, and mutual support purposes. This immigration wave was economic.

The second wave was political and took place during the Communist regime in Bulgaria and the era of the Cold War. Emigration and communities abroad were influenced by the then Bulgarian policy that all those who didn't accept and support the new regime were declared enemies of the people. During this period, the Bulgarian party and the government put a great deal of pressure on the established organizations abroad, but despite the attempts for "native" influence, these organizations did not change.

To mark the 1300th anniversary of the founding of Bulgaria, the church attempted to reach out to established Orthodox organizations abroad by establishing a diocese in Budapest. The main objective of the party was to succeed in securing its position in the country and establishing contact with the Western bloc.

Political unrest in Bulgaria after 1989 and the freedom of people to leave the country marked the third wave, a new period in the organization and development of Bulgarian communities and their organizations abroad. This migration was radically new; the main motive was foreign realization—temporary or permanent or education. Rather, we are no longer talking about migration, but about mobility.

This also affected companies formed in this new period, which were not political or economic, but rather organizations that help preserve the spiritual identity of migrants. Sunday schools, folk groups, and centers were established. The interesting thing about this period is that the host society also accepted these traditions and rituals.

As an example, I can use the folklore ensemble Zornitsa created by Tatyana Serbinska—founder and conductor of the ensemble and the women's choir Wild Women. The participants are mostly American musicians and performers captivated by the charm of Bulgarian folklore. They take an active part in the cultural life of the Bulgarian community in North America and participate in elite folk festivals and festivals in

Bulgaria. Zdravets is another well-known ensemble created by Marta Forsythe, a woman who has spent much of her life preserving and spreading Bulgarian culture in North America. The establishment and maintenance of these organizations helps preserve the Bulgarian spiritual heritage in the second and subsequent generations of emigrants.

Bulgarian authors present authentic folklore dances, rituals, and exhibitions. Theater productions and concerts increase the desire of these new generations born abroad to become acquainted with Bulgarian culture. The number of courses, dance groups, and theater groups is also increasing.

Folklore Ensemble "Crazy Young," created by Peter Petrov in Boston, is one of the leaders in the spread of folk dance; the ensemble regularly participates in prestigious competitions and festivals. They help raise funds and support Bulgarian organizations. Interest in folklore dance is increasing not only among Bulgarians but also among the host community.

Cultural centers are a beacon that diffuse light and rally Bulgarians abroad. The main characteristic element of these centers is not only to organize celebrations, but also to attract and invite artists and performers from Bulgaria. These centers are numerous not only in Europe but also in North America. Behind each one stands a patriot or a group of patriots, in most cases volunteers.

One of these centers is Madara, created by my friend Violeta Zhelyazkova. Our lives crossed paths in 1998, the year I moved to New England with my family. With her help and that of other Bulgarians, we were able to start building our lives abroad. Vili is a girl with a big heart, a lot of energy, and most importantly, an unrequited love for Bulgaria. I call her "Spark."

With her help, the idea of "BG Mass" was born and later grew into the "Madara Bulgarian-American Cultural Center," which is still the main pillar of the Bulgarian community in New England. It all started one meeting when a group of people gathered because of our love of Bulgaria. It's difficult to describe in a few lines what lies behind the creation and construction of this organization. I'll only share that it's like raising a child: it needs love, patience, and forgiveness.

Vili put a lot of effort into this center, which unites and gathers Bulgarians on national holidays, picnics, charity events, festivals, exhibitions, and concerts. I haven't kept statistics, but the center has initiated and facilitated more than 500 community events in the US and Canada. Thanks to the center, Boston and North America have hosted the biggest Bulgarian pop and theater stars, talented artists, and musicians. For this reason, new generations born abroad have become acquainted with Bulgarian culture and values, and have become familiar with their identity.

In addition, Vili also participates in the creation and management of other Bulgarian centers in the area—the Bulgarian church "St. Petka," our school "St. Cyril and Methodius," and the Bulgarian Center in New England. Not surprisingly, in 2018, Vili was distinguished with the highest honor, "Order of Ivan Vazov," for her work in preserving Bulgarian spirituality and culture abroad. In addition, she's received an honorary diploma from Massachusetts Governor, Charlie Baker, and has received many other accolades. More than 400 people attended the celebration to pay their respect and love for Vili. A photo of her and her husband, Georgi Enchev, is at the Museum Exposition Dream of Freedom, reflecting the history of Bulgarian emigration in Boston. The exposition is located in the most-visited tourist spot in the city—Skywalk Observatory, Prudential Center.

Patriotism and maintaining Bulgaria abroad is in her blood and family history. Vili's relatives are Patricia Penka French and Galina Kurteva, who also engage in active community service on the US east coast.

Patricia Penka French was a longtime president of one of the first Bulgarian centers in the United States—the Bulgarian-Macedonian National Educational and Cultural Center—in Pittsburgh, Pennsylvania, and the director of development of the Bulgarian Tambouritza Folk Ensemble. She donated much to the cause of arts and culture and was an energetic and tireless advocate for Bulgarian culture in the US until her death on January 12, 2019.

Galina Kurteva is the president of Alpha Art Gallery in New Brunswick, New Jersey. Ms. Kurteva and her husband, artist Veselin Kurtev, opened the first gallery in the New Jersey area, which promotes the work of Bulgarian artists, along with that of American artists. Galina and Veselin's gallery also hosts many exciting Bulgarian events, making it the center of Bulgarians in the area.

I've mentioned only some of the outstanding people I've met, but many others give their time and energy to preserving and spreading Bulgarian culture abroad. In this book I've mentioned that, for me, "immigrant" is a word that is outdated in today's world without borders. We must not think that a nation is enclosed "within the boundaries" of a country. Bulgarians abroad should be seen as an integral part of any nation. Their cultural practices should fit and be recorded into the heritage of that country, because we are part of a global nation. Sunday schools, cultural centers, amateur folk groups, churches, and other well-known and unknown community organizations contribute to the preservation of Bulgarian spirituality.

Thanks to all those patriots who keep the flame alive and bring light and love into the lives of Bulgarians abroad.

Glossary

Aizmo: holy water at a sacred church or sanctuary
Asma: a wooden or metal structure like a pergola to support a climbing grapevine
Baba: grandmother
Baklitsa, **baklitsi** (plural): wooden vessel for wine
Banitsa: egg-and-cheese-filled pastry made from filo dough
Bogovitza: round bread made on Budni vecher, Christmas Eve
Budnik: a log burned on Budni vecher
Cheshma: fountain at a well or spring
Hamkane: a red thread with a piece of halva, cheese, or a hard-boiled egg tied to it
Horo: circle dance
Kachamak: traditional Bulgarian dish made with milk, layers of fried pork, butter, and cheese
Kalushari: group of men who have been taught magical, healing arts
Karakondjula, **karakonjuli** (plural): evil night spirit
Katun: a group of gypsy families who travel together
Kaval: long flute-like instrument, a shepherd's pipe
Kazan: place where rakia brandy is made
Kenar: handmade material, a mixture of cotton and silk
Khan: small motel or inn
Kozunak: traditional Easter ritual sweet bread
Kumov kravai: richly decorated wedding bread
Kvas: a fermented mixture of flour, salt, and water, like a starter dough
Lamia: evil female dragon
Lazarka, **lazarki** (plural): girls who sing around the village on Lazarovden, St. Lazar's Day
Locum: a common sweet used in rituals
Lukanka: appetizer similar to Italian dry salami
Martenitsa, **martenitsi** (plural): red and white amulet
Nestinari: fire dancers

Noshtvie: a wooden vessel that looks like a trough
Obrok: sacred place
Orisia: destiny
Oristnizi: three Fates who visit newborns to determine their future
Paraklis: special bread baked on St. Nikolas' Day
Pitka: round, ritual soda bread
Podnitza: round, earthen dish used to cook on coals
Pogacha: a ritual to celebrate the birth of a child
Prostupulnik: a ritual that determines a child's future profession
Rakia: home-made brandy
Ruchenitz: fast horo dance
Rusalka, **rusalki** (plural): female water spirit, often called a mermaid
Samodiva, **samodivi** (plural): woodland nymph or fairy
Sedianka: gathering of women
Sharena sol (colorful salt): a mixture of herbs, red pepper, and salt
Sirnizi: branches for a bonfire
Stomna: pottery vessel used to carry water
Stopan: guardian spirit
Survachka, **survachki** (plural): decorated dogwood stick
Talasum: spirit created by burying a person or animal into a wall to act as a protector of a place
Tupan: drum
Urochasan: a state of being cursed by the "evil eye"
Uroki: evil spirits, or the "evil eye"
Zasiavka: wedding bread
Zdravets: Bulgarian geranium
Zmey: male dragon
Znahar, **znahari** (plural): herbal or folk healer

About the Author

Ronesa Aveela is "the creative power of two." Two authors that is. The main force behind the work, the creative genius, was born in Bulgaria and moved to the US in the 1990s. She grew up with stories of wild Samodivi, Kikimora, the dragons Zmey and Lamia, Baba Yaga, and much more. She's a freelance artist and writer. She likes writing mystery romance inspired by legends and tales. In her free time, she paints. Her artistic interests include the female figure, Greek and Thracian mythology, folklore tales, and the natural world interpreted through her eyes. She is married and has two children.

Her writing partner was born and raised in the New England area. She has a background in writing and editing, as well as having a love of all things from different cultures. She's learned so much about Bulgarian culture, folklore, and rituals, and writes to share that knowledge with others.

Connect with Us!

Website: http://ronesaaveela.com/

Go to our website to find more social media links: our newsletter, Facebook, Twitter, Instagram, Pinterest, Goodreads, BookBub, LinkedIn, and YouTube. Or promo products on Redbubble: https://www.redbubble.com/people/aveela

Ronesa's Books

Fiction
Mystical Emona: Soul's Journey
The Unborn Hero of Dragon Village
Zmeykovo (Bulgarian version of *The Unborn Hero of Dragon Village*)

La profezia del Villaggio del Drago (Italian version of *The Unborn Hero of Dragon Village*)

Nonfiction
Light Love Rituals: Bulgarian Myths, Legends, and Folklore
The Wanderer – A Tear and A Smile: Reflections of an Immigrant
Skitnikut - usmivki I sulzi: Rasmisleniata na edin bulgarski emigrant
    (Bulgarian version of *The Wanderer*)
A Study of Household Spirits of Eastern Europe
A Study of Rusalki – Slavic Mermaids of Eastern Europe
A Study of Vodyanoy – Water Spirit of Eastern Europe
    (Free gift when you sign up for our newsletter:
    https://dl.bookfunnel.com/1rq3ku0fa9)

Children's short stories, activity & coloring books
Baba Treasure Chest series
The Christmas Thief
The Miracle Stork
Born From the Ashes
Mermaid's Gift
Baba Treasure Chest: A Collection of Modern Bulgarian Tales
(contains all four short stories)

Coloring Books
Mermaids Around the World
More Mermaids Around the World
Little Zoi

Cookbook
Mediterranean & Bulgarian Cuisine: 12 Easy Traditional Favorites

Reviews

PLEASE HELP AUTHORS BY LEAVING A REVIEW!
We hope you've enjoyed this book, and that its illustrations and words have inspired you. As an author with a small publisher, we would appreciate your gift of a review. Good or bad, we'd love to hear your honest thoughts.

www.ingramcontent.com/pod-product-compliance
Lightning Source LLC
Chambersburg PA
CBHW041129110526
44592CB00020B/2734